Online Auctions!

I Didn't Know You Could Do That...™

Bruce Frey

SYBEX®

San Francisco • Paris • Düsseldorf • Soest • London

Associate Publisher: Cheryl Applewood
Contracts and Licensing Manager: Kristine O'Callaghan
Acquisitions and Developmental Editor: Sherry Bonelli
Editors: Kathy Grider-Carlyle, Brianne Agatep
Production Editor: Leslie E. H. Light
Book Designers: Franz Baumhackl, Kate Kaminski
Electronic Publishing Specialist: Kris Warrenburg
Proofreader: Nancy Riddiough
Indexer: Carol Burbo
CD Technicians: Keith McNeil, Siobhan Dowling
CD Coordinator: Kara Eve Schwartz
Cover Designer: Daniel Ziegler
Cover and Chapter Photographs: PhotoDisc

Library of Congress Card Number: 00-106233

ISBN: 0-7821-2708-8

Acknowledgments

Thanks to Bonnie, Nona, and Neil for their help and support. Special thanks to Lester Dent, Laird Cregar, and Chuck Taine.

The author also wishes to thank the folks at Sybex: Cheryl Applewood, Brianne Agatep, Leslie E.H. Light, Kathy Grider-Carlyle, Nancy Riddiough, Keith McNeil, Kara Schwartz, Carol Burbo, Kris Warrenburg and all the nameless, faceless others for their help.

Contents

Introduction

I am a collector.

As a teenager, I collected comic books. I liked the Superman and Batman stories published by DC comics, not the Spider-Man and Fantastic Four stories published by Marvel. Marvel stories always continued from issue to issue, and the superheroes would fight with each other all the time. This was not the way I thought superheroes should behave. (And, of course, it isn't!)

As an adult, I collect just about everything. I like animation art, original comic book art, first edition books, Big Little Books, memorabilia related to the great magician Houdini, paperback novelizations of 1960s and 1970s TV shows (like *Man from Uncle, Dark Shadows,* and the *Partridge Family*), comic books (still), and most importantly to me, I collect all things relating to Doc Savage, the Man of Bronze. Doc was a fictional hero of the pulp magazines from the 1930s and 1940s and was reprinted in about 175 paperback novels in the 1960s and 1970s. There was a movie (and, perhaps, another on the way), plenty of advertising premiums, comic books, and radio shows. So, there is plenty to collect.

There is plenty to buy and plenty to sell. I sell when I need more money to buy more collectibles, or when I have some item I have no interest in, like a duplicate or something that I must have been crazy to think I would want to keep for the rest of my life. (Are you interested in my Bo Jackson rookie baseball card?) Until recently, it was tough to find Doc Savage collectibles for sale and even harder to find a place to sell Doc Savage collectibles. Collectibles weren't my business, just my hobby, and it was hard to find anyone with whom to trade. Then came eBay.

I stumbled across eBay five years ago—before the hype—maybe before you did. eBay was the first live, large scale, online auction service. It focused on collectibles, but all sorts of new and used non-collectibles were available, too. On eBay, you could bid on so much different stuff (and I am talking about items that you always thought were rare because the antique mall in your town never offered them) that you thought you'd died and gone to heaven (or in the case of Doc Savage, his Fortress of Solitude at the Arctic Circle).

That first day I bid on a dozen auctions, bids amounting to hundreds of dollars. Some I actually won. Not all, thank goodness, as I didn't have hundreds of dollars. A memorable early win was the original art for the cover of a *Betty and Veronica* comic book. I wasn't the only one with memorable buying experiences. Over the years, newly discovered Masters, the world's most-valuable baseball card, and even the Declaration of Independence have been auctioned off on the Internet. Soon, I was selling, too. Because I found that what I had bought on impulse I quickly lost interest in, especially as I noticed that similar items were being offered almost daily, and going for less. (Are you interested in my original art for the cover of a *Betty and Veronica* comic book? It's still in the original shrink-wrap….) I sold items for a profit that I purchased cheap on eBay. I sold items that I had purchased elsewhere and no longer wanted. I learned a lot and got better at it.

Dozens of competitors since then have joined eBay. Some big names run online auction sites. Yahoo! and Amazon among others—eBay is by far the biggest, Amazon is making a run at it, and Yahoo! has a huge potential base of users to challenge.

Along with buying, thousands of individuals run selling businesses entirely on the Internet, using online auction sites as their primary, or only, Web sites. A variety of different types of people sell on eBay, Yahoo!, and Amazon. Which are you?

◆ A collector who has a collectible that you want to sell for as much as you can get. You will use the money to buy more stuff for your own collection.

◆ An individual who wants to make a little extra money by selling stuff at auction online. Some are collectibles; some are items you picked-up with the express purpose of selling at a profit. Some money you'll keep for other uses; some you'll spend on your hobby.

◆ A business that sells from home—through the Internet, through advertisements, but entirely through the mail.

◆ A traditional business that has a storefront. You sell in-person and through the mail. You may use your auctions to sell collectibles, though you might also sell more useful products like computers, electronics, and used books.

If you see yourself in one of these categories, this book is for you.

Online Auctions! I Didn't Know You Could Do That... is an in-depth look at the strategy and philosophy of buying and selling at online auction sites. This is not an introductory book. We assume that you have some experience either buying or selling at a site, but you want to learn and think more about making the right choices while you are there. The three largest online auction sites (eBay, Amazon, and Yahoo!) are discussed—although the bulk of the action is at eBay and the bulk of this book uses eBay as the example in discussions.

The central premise of *Online Auctions! I Didn't Know You Could Do That...* is that an online auction is a game. Like any game, there are strategies and tactics. There is a way to play to win. For the seller, winning the game means making money. If you have a book at home about how to win at chess or in poker or in the stock market (or even how to win at *Pokémon: The Trading Card Game*), then place this book on the same shelf.

My teaching plan is to:

1. Take you through the mind of a buyer and a seller.

2. Examine all the aspects of buying and selling. What options are available and how should we think about them to make our decisions?

3. Provide detailed how-to instructions on some of the more technical requirements for good selling. How do I include a picture? How do I link to a Web site? How do I put those cute, blinking eyes in my listing? Or, better yet, *should* I put those cute, blinking eyes in my listing?

4. Talk to the experts. I've asked successful, online auction buyers and sellers to share their thoughts about buying, selling, listing, and providing customer service.

5. Examine the different sides of the issues. Like any game, online auctions has its devotees to different strategies, which sometimes conflict. Do you want your bidders to bid early or late? When is it worth it to include a picture? When should you leave feedback?

6. Provide the tools you need. One of the coolest things in this book is the CD-ROM, which contains some of the best auction utilities you've seen listed on eBay, Yahoo!, and Amazon.

If I succeed in meeting these six goals, then this book should be a useful addition to your games book shelf, right between Sun-Tzu's *Art of War* and de Firmian's *Modern Chess Openings*.

One more thing. Although you are allowed to buy and sell almost anything legal on eBay, Amazon, and Yahoo!, the beauty, strength, and history of these sites comes from the buying and selling of collectibles. This book tends to use examples from the world of collecting. Don't fear, though. You will still gain as much from this book if you are selling 1/2-inch washers, but the examples are more likely to mention a rare, hardback 1933 edition of the Doc Savage novel *Land of Fear* in very good condition than they are to mention 1/2-inch washers. I don't want you to feel neglected, though. As you have likely discovered, much of the buying and selling at these sites is of non-collectibles—new or used, but still useful, items that we use everyday like games, books, videos, CDs, clothing, electronic equipment, cameras, and so forth. We will always take time to discuss any special wrinkles or different ways of thinking that apply to auctions of non-collectibles. Fortunately for us, the tips and strategies tend to be the same regardless of what is being auctioned.

Good luck. The game is afoot. (And I'm serious about the Bo Jackson card. I'd let it go for half of guide. Let me know.)

How Is This Book Organized?

This book is divided into parts. Each part is a collection of numbered sections that focus on key components of the online auction buying and selling process for the three major sites: eBay, Yahoo!, and Amazon.

Buying Starts Here   This part provides an advanced examination of the basics when bidding. We talk about budgeting, figuring out how much to bid, taking into account hidden costs, buying collectibles as an investment, investigating sellers before you bid, analyzing listings, and protecting yourself when you buy.

Bidding to Win   Here you'll be treated to a more in-depth look at the strategy and tactics of bidding, ways to *win* the game, not just play. Topics include determining the *real* value of an auction item, using price guides, *sniping* (bidding at the last second), using bidding software, recognizing shady sellers and shill bidding, and smoothly completing a transaction.

Buying into the Online Community   This part discusses the buyer's obligations and opportunities as a member of the online auction community, as well as record-keeping options. Choices and strategies for leaving feedback, keeping track of auctions, and how to learn more about the things you buy from the sellers who run the auctions are among the areas presented.

Power Selling Starts Here   Here we begin to analyze the basics of selling at online auctions. We look at budgeting when running auctions, choosing your favorite definition of *profit*, paying attention to hidden selling costs, determining Web site fees at eBay, Amazon, and Yahoo!, and investigating the high bidder before the auction ends.

Selling to Win   This part suggests more specific strategies when making choices as a seller. Among the topics discussed here are setting a reserve price, comparing different auction formats, designing auctions that end only when the bids have stopped, choosing a starting minimum bid, communicating with bidders, recognizing shill bidding and shady bidders, and choosing the auction site for you.

Closing the Sale   Here we focus on the moments near the end of an auction and right after an auction ends. Strategic choices can help you spot potential problems. You'll learn how to collect information about your winning bidders, increase future sales, communicate with buyers, and use software for record-keeping and communication. You'll also learn how to choose a feedback philosophy.

Making the Exchange   This part is dedicated to the very important matters of getting paid and shipping the item (in that order). Accepting checks, dealing with credit cards, using escrow to protect buyer and seller, choosing shipping options, and packaging are among the topics covered.

Designing a Killer Listing   This part of the book presents all the details, tricks, and tips for auction design. We get a little technical here as we look at the information presented in auction listings on all three major Web sites. You'll learn how to choose a name for your auction that includes *hot button* words and write a complete and powerful item description. You'll get the scoop on making and attaching photos to your listings, identifying and pasting the locations of photos into your listing, and using software to design listings. You'll learn more HTML formatting tricks than you can shake a mouse at, including the entire HTML code for a simple and effective auction listing and ways to upload a whole bunch of auction listings at one time.

Your Name on the Shingle   Here we present the policy and business decisions sellers can make with an emphasis on quality customer service. Among the areas we examine are choosing what to sell, tapping into the variety of support for sellers that can be found online, tracking the competition, choosing the best sales policies, and choosing whether or not to trade internationally.

Selling into the Online Community   This closes out our discussions by looking at the role of the seller in the online auction society. Among other things, you'll be reminded to follow the rules, take part in eBay's elaborate system of social support and other online services, consider using certification services for your collectibles, and learn from your customers.

Bruce Frey

Buying Starts
Here

The premise for this book is that online auctions can be analyzed as a game, and winning strategies can be developed as they can for any game. Both bidders and sellers can be winners in this game. *Online Auctions! I Didn't Know You Could Do That…* presents advance strategies, analyses, tips, tricks, and a healthy amount of opinion to help all players win. (By the way, every player in this game *can* come out a winner. Pretty good deal!)

Before we look at how to win as online auction sellers, we first need to look at how to win as online auction buyers. Even if you only want to *sell* at auction online, and leave the bidding to collectors and bargain hunters like the rest of us, there are good reasons to spend some time discussing the buying process:

◆ A winning online seller understands his customer. By learning how to win as an online auction buyer, you can understand your customers' mindset by finding out firsthand what customers want, what they look for, and how they make decisions.

◆ By walking through the steps and decisions as a bidder, you can remind yourself about the important parts of an auction. Later in the book, I'll examine these components to help you devise a winning selling strategy.

◆ Online auction sellers are almost always also auction buyers You may buy items at auction and then resell them for profit. The nature of collectibles is such that they can go up in value, sometimes quite quickly. With some hard work and a little luck, you can actually buy low and sell high. Not a bad strategy. (Those are the sort of gems of wisdom you'll get in this book. Jot it down: "Buy low and sell high." You heard it here first!)

N O T E   This book is ideal for buyers and sellers of collectibles, but it is also for those who want to buy or sell most anything that is sold at eBay, Yahoo!, or Amazon. Although the strategies for selling to a high bid or buying with a low bid tend to be the same regardless of the actual item being auctioned, some of the other ins and outs of the online auction world take on a different flavor for non-collectibles (e.g., clothing, cameras, and computers) than they do for collectibles (e.g., Beanie Babies, comic books, and sports cards). Where appropriate, I've emphasized these distinctions.

NOTE Defining *collectibles* is a little like defining *obscenity*: It is hard to define, but you know it when you see it. Almost any definition excludes many perfectly good examples of collectibles. I once heard an appraiser define collectibles as "anything you have more of than you need" and that seems to work well. Let's think of a collectible as anything you happen to collect.

This part of the book talks about buying on a budget, figuring out the real costs, locating sources of items to sell, and determining the quality of the *seller*. A quality seller provides good service and a good product at a good price.

1 Budgeting when Buying

So, you've decided to hunt for buried treasure on an online auction site? If you're eager to get straight to the power-selling stuff and are reading this buying section only to be polite, just play along and keep reading. I promise that reading this section will be worth your time! Buying costs money. So, even if you are lucky enough to find the 1992 Norman Rockwell Mother's Day plate, how much can you afford to pay for it? This is a different question than "How much should I bid for it?" Let's give some thought to these questions.

WARNING One basic issue you should consider is how much money you can afford to spend buying online. As a collector, you need to determine your spending limit *before* you start bidding, and as a bargain hunter, you need to know what really is a good deal. Auctions are exciting. It's easy to get caught up in the excitement and bid more on an item than you should or, as commonly happens, bid in *more* auctions than you can afford *and* find yourself hoping that you don't win them all.

How Much Should I Pay?

People buy something at an online auction for one of three reasons. They plan to:

◆ Resell it

◆ Keep it for themselves (to use or collect)

◆ Give it as a gift

If you are buying in order to resell, the goal should be to make a profit, and the best strategy is to buy for less than you will eventually sell it for. The trick, of course, is to accurately predict what to buy, when to resell, and how long it will take before values increase enough for selling to make sense.

NOTE Knowing the likely resale value of an item is discussed in greater detail later. See number 3, "Buying from Peter to Sell to Paul," number 5, "What Is It Worth?," and number 20, "Aren't I Supposed to Make a Profit? Maybe…"

If you are buying an item at auction in order to get it for less than you would pay elsewhere, calculating how much you should pay is fairly simple—pay less than it costs elsewhere, obviously. However, if you are buying an item to keep as a collectible or give as a gift, knowing how much to pay is much more difficult. How much to pay is really a psychological question because its value mainly comes from the satisfaction of owning it or giving it to someone else. The following steps will help you decide exactly, to the penny, how much to pay:

1. Don't bid the moment you find an item that excites you. If an auction isn't ending in the next few minutes, take a bit of time to see if your enthusiasm subsides before committing yourself to bidding.

2. To zero in on your bid amount, decide your theoretical (imaginary) upper limit. This is the amount that you can *responsibly* afford to pay for this item. If you have debts, bills to pay, or some other grown-up use for the money, don't bid. This advice is worth repeating. Do not spend more time or money on eBay, Amazon, or Yahoo! than you can afford. The Internet is supposed to be fun. Like the government, it is "here to help you," so don't let it hurt you!

3. Now you know your theoretical upper limit. Begin to lower that amount until you reach the amount that is psychologically comfortable for you. What is its empirical (in your world) value? This is the amount of money you are willing to give to someone else so that you can have that item in your own hot, little hands. Lower and raise this amount in your mind until you emotionally "feel" that there is equality.

4. Now fine-tune that figure to a precise dollar amount, out to two decimals. If you are willing to pay $35, are you willing to pay $35.50? How about $35.51? Bidders who aren't as good at the game as you are will probably bid in round numbers. Your extra few pennies can make the difference.

5. Now that you have an exact figure that you want to pay (in total), subtract the postage and packaging costs quoted in the listing. This is real money that adds to the real cost, and you have already decided the exact maximum amount you want to pay, so it doesn't make sense to add the postage on to that amount. The smaller the winning bid, the bigger the bite, proportionately speaking, that postage can take.

This final number is the most you should bid. It is your *magic number*. Do not go over that amount. If you lose the auction, you still win the game, because you were able to bid exactly the right amount. Someone else wanted it a little more—that's all. There are more buried treasures to dig up and more great deals to find.

How Much Should I Bid?

Online auctions allow you to enter a *maximum bid amount*. The value of a computer-controlled auction is that you don't have to be there for the actual bidding. You tell the computer (at Amazon, Yahoo!, or eBay) how much you are willing to pay. In your name, the site computer then raises the current bid on the item automatically to the next *bid increment* if your maximum bid is higher than the current bid. Bid increments are small increases based on traditional dollar amounts that old-fashioned auctions have used for years. The increment gets bigger as the dollar amount of the highest bid increases. Because the computer knows the maximum bids of all the other bidders, it "bids" on their behalf, increasing, as appropriate, using these bid increments. Your bid will be raised to the level of your maximum bid only if necessary to outbid someone else.

NOTE Even though bid increments are mandated by the bidding systems of the auction services, the strategy of bidding to the exact penny will still help you win auctions. When the maximum bid is a tie, the earliest bidder wins. If your maximum bid is a penny more, then there is no tie. The bid amount will reflect that exact penny figure, even if that figure seems impossible according to the bid increment rules.

I recommend that you enter the *magic number* you calculated earlier as your maximum bid. There is some debate over when you should do this (early on or at the very last minute), which I'll discuss later, but no harm can come by following the steps and entering this number as your maximum bid. Tables 1.1 and 1.2 list bidding increments for eBay, Amazon, and Yahoo!

TABLE 1.1   Bid Increase Increments for eBay and Amazon

Current Bid	Increment
$0–$0.99	$0.05
$1–$4.99	$0.25
$5–$24.99	$0.50
$25–$99.99	$1
$100–$249.99	$2
$250–$499.99	$5
$500–$999.99	$10
$1,000–$2499.99	$25
$2,500–$4999.99	$50
$5,000 and up	$100

TABLE 1.2   Bid Increase Increments for Yahoo!

Current Bid	Increment
$0–$10	$0.10
$10.01–$50	$1
$50.01–$100	$2.50
$100.01–$500	$5
$500.01 and up	$10

2   Finding the Hidden Costs when Buying

I've already talked about remembering the added costs of postage and packaging for your purchases, but there are other potential costs to be concerned about.

Additional Costs

Let's look at some of the common charges beyond the winning bid amount that buyers are asked to include in their payment.

Shipping   This is the expected, actual cost of putting postage on a package or envelope and having it delivered, and it is almost always required by the seller. Postage can be as little as the cost of a stamp; but for heavy objects, big objects, and items sent to (as my father used to say) "other lands," shipping can be very expensive.

Handling   As in "shipping and handling," this phrase usually means "picking and packing." Handling is the cost of retrieving the item from inventory and packaging it up. Sometimes, however, the word is used to collect money for the time and trouble it takes to mail an item or run an online auction. Collecting money for postage and the cost of the packaging is reasonable, but in my opinion, additional costs due to time, employees, storage, and so on are the cost of doing business and should be reflected in the *asking price*. In online auctions, the asking price is the *starting price* or, if it's a *reserve auction*, the asking price is the *reserve price*, the lowest bid for which you will sell the item. I don't mind rounding off this cost, but handling costs shouldn't be an opportunity to charge massive additional fees.

NOTE Keep in mind that if a winning bid is very low, any additional fees, even if reasonable, may seem high because they may be more than the amount of the winning bid. That, by itself, doesn't mean the fees are unreasonable.

Packaging Usually, some cost is incurred by the seller for the packing materials, and this can be more than just a few pennies for well-packed or unusually shaped items. Larger items—and items requiring special packaging—typically have larger packaging costs. It is common for sellers to charge an additional fee to cover this expense.

NOTE Some methods of shipment do not add costs for the package itself. Priority Mail though the U.S. Postal Service, for example, includes a free box.

Regarding packaging costs, you may be more price savvy than the seller. Big stuff, like furniture and large paintings, requires bulky packaging. Novice sellers may be unaware of packaging needs and extra costs. Be prepared to pay more than a few extra dollars and offer suggestions about shipping options.

Listing A troubling trend of the last year is the still rare, but growing, practice of charging the buyer for the cost of listing the auction on the Web site. This is ridiculous! When you go into a showroom to buy a new car, the salesman doesn't tell you that in addition to the sticker price you must pay the cost of the car company's expensive ad during the Super Bowl. The sticker price should already include all the tangential costs of doing business. If you see an auction that requires payment of a listing fee, avoid that seller. That's what I do.

Optional Costs

These additional costs are often offered as choices you can make for a small extra fee. When the cost is small, you should consider them. Consider the availability of these options as a sign of a quality seller who cares about the buyer (you!). Your optional cost can include:

Insurance   Many sellers offer postal insurance to cover the risk of damage or loss during mailing. If you can pay this cost without going over your magic number, consider doing so. Problems are rare (which is how the postal service and other companies make money on this option), but decide whether the extra money is worth the extra peace of mind. When deciding whether or not to buy insurance, be sure to consider the uniqueness of the item and whether it can be replaced at all. With collectibles, for example, items are often one-of-a-kind. Insurance covers replacement value only, not sentimental value. If the item is destroyed or missing, perhaps a little insurance payout will ease the pain a bit, even though it won't replace the item.

WARNING The United States Postal Service requires a receipt, or other business records evidence, to prove value before it will honor the amount you have written on the insurance form. Think of the declared value as the *most* the post office will pay. Without proof of value, you will get (at best) less than that amount, or (at worst) nothing at all!

NOTE Postal insurance providers other than the U.S. Postal Service are available. You may find them cheaper and easier to use. Consider services offered by providers like Universal Parcel Insurance Coverage at www.u-pic.com (which is endorsed by the U.S.P.S. and covers all modes of freight, including UPS, FedEx, etc.) or Parcel Insurance Plan at www.pipinsure.com.

Safer and Quicker Mailing   You can mail through Priority Mail, United Parcel Service, Federal Express, and a variety of other carriers, which allow for quicker or more secure delivery. Some sellers allow, or even require, that you use these services, and there will be additional costs. If the seller requires you to use a more expensive service than regular mail, decide if you are still willing to buy with the added costs.

Overhead Costs

You can accrue additional costs just by being online and paying by check or credit card. Decide if these costs should be considered part of your buying costs. They may be substantial for you or meaningless; the key is to be aware of them and consider how they affect you.

Internet Costs   It costs you *something* to be online. Not only is there the associated cost of computers and Internet access, but there is also the value of the time you spend browsing, searching, and buying online. You can decrease or eliminate many of these costs, by the way. There are providers of free Internet service, for example. Check out www.isps-free.com, www.freeatlast.com, and www.netzero.com, just to name a few. Also, auction management applications like those on this book's CD, will save you loads of time, and your time is worth something. Isn't it?

Banking Costs   Does it cost you money to write a check? Buying a money order or cashier's check can be costly, too. Count these fees toward your purchase cost. Some sellers require money orders and do not accept checks. Using a credit card costs money too. Many of the larger online auction sellers accept credit cards and using them may be convenient, but there are associated costs involved—monthly interest and possibly yearly fees. If you charge a $100 winning bid and do not pay it off in a month, you have actually won the item for a bid greater than $100.

WARNING   Using credits cards can provide greater convenience for buyers, but using them also offers a greater opportunity to add to the cost of bidding. Tread carefully!

Whoops! More Costs

My experiences, and those of almost everyone I know, have been uniformly positive when buying at online auction sites. Rarely, though, buying does not go smoothly, and the bumps in the road can sometimes cost you money. You will hardly ever have to pay the costs listed here, but it never hurts to be aware of these possibilities:

Additional Postage   Occasionally, not often, the transaction won't go smoothly, and you may have to send an additional letter or return a package.

Additional Banking Costs   You may need to send a replacement check for one that's been lost or stop payment for a lost check.

Registered Mailing Costs   If the worst scenario occurs, or you are overly cautious, you may need to send a letter that requires signature upon receipt. This costs money.

Legal Costs   I've never had to hire a lawyer for an online transaction gone bad, but with millions of transactions weekly, I'm sure someone has.

Few of these costs will ever impact your life as an auction trader, but certainly you will need to pay postage and handling, and occasionally insurance or the cost of priority mail. So, be aware, count it as real money, and adjust your *magic number* accordingly.

3 Buying from Peter to Sell to Paul

Earlier I talked about three reasons to buy online auction style. One of those reasons was to buy with the hope of reselling your purchase at some later time to make a profit. The idea of collectibles as an investment is what drives many buyers. It's worth pointing out that there is an important distinction between collecting, investing, and *speculating*. Collectors collect and are unconcerned about whether the monetary value of their collection increases or decreases. Investors put their money to work, planning to earn interest or otherwise make a profit. Investor profits usually come slowly over a long period of time. Speculators, on the other hand, are bigger gamblers than investors, relying on wide swings in the value of what they own. They hope to make their profit quickly, over a shorter period of time, and hope to make a lot of it. Many buyers of collectibles think of themselves as a little bit of all three of these types of people. Online auctions provide many opportunities for collectors, very few opportunities for investors (unless you buy stock in the companies themselves), and a moderate amount of opportunities for speculators. If you live the auction life mostly as a speculator, and are proud of it, this section is for you.

Hot Collectibles

Take a look at a few of the hottest collectible areas over the last decade or so. Each of these areas got a lot of publicity, some more than others, and generated a great deal of excitement. Will they stand the test of time, like Barbies, or wither away like Pogs (if you don't know, don't ask)? Some of these areas have already begun to cool, and by the time you read this book, a whole new area is likely to have emerged.

Pokémon   At this writing, the Pokémon craze is in full bloom. There is a hit movie with sequels already in the pipeline, a TV cartoon show, fast food giveaways, toys, and—most important to 10-year-old investors—trading cards. Kids buy the cards partly to play with as components in a fun card game, but also with the idea that they will go up in value and can be resold for a profit. For this reason, many cards are left untouched and unopened, lest they lose their mint condition. Of course, this teaches our children gambling, not investing. But who can talk sense to 100 screaming tykes demanding three unopened packs of cards for their five bucks? You'll find tons of Pokémon listings on auction Web sites, many resulting in sales above retail.

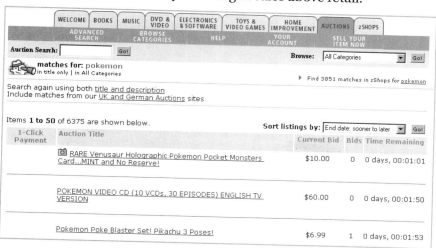

Beanie Babies Very young children learned how to be investors instead of collectors by watching their parents go crazy for these cute stuffed animals. Legend has it that at some point, demand became so high that the creatures went up in value. Limited editions, which had true scarcity, followed and the mass hysteria wasn't far behind. If you sense that I am cynical of these sorts of *investments* where a 7-year-old girl is told that she can't play with Seaweed, the adorable stuffed otter that Mom just bought because it may go up in value, then you are right. Of course, most parent collectors of Beanies Babies buy more than one copy, so their kids can actually play with them, but you get the point. (And yes, I know, Seaweed has held his value admirably, and he is cute. Have you seen him? He is cuddling a teeny little piece of green seaweed and has the sweetest, most adorable look in his eyes and…um…guess we better move on.) In terms of the number of auction listings and number of buyers and sellers, Beanie Babies are one of the hottest categories in the world of online auctions.

Magic: The Gathering Cards You may not have heard of these collectible cards, but the students at your local high school or college have. Magic is a card game where you battle an opponent.

Category Listing	Title Only	Description Only

Category Search Results for **Beanie Babies** (1 items)

Auctions > Toys & Games > Beanbag Collectibles > Ty Products > Beanie Babies

Title Search Results for **Beanie Babies** (1805 items)

Showing **1** of **37** pages(1805 items total)   [Show only photos]   Previous 50 | Next 50

Photo	Title	Current Bid	Bids	▲ Time Left
	Featured Auctions (more info)			
	12 Valentina Beanie Babies, Buy price of $54, cc ok, seller rating 230+	$54.00	2	2 hrs
	Clubby II Beanie Babie and Buddy, Retired and Mint Condition	$29.99	-	2 hrs
📷	K I C K S Beanie Babie Shipped Tag Protected In Mint Condition .	$6.00	3	5 hrs
📷	O S I T O The Mexican Beanie Babie Shipped Tag Protected(3 Available)	$9.00	1	17 hrs
	1997 Complete Set (10) McDonalds Teenie Beanie Babies TBB MIP	$70.00	-	1 day
	1998 Complete Set (12) McDonalds Teenie Beanie Babies TBB MIP	$26.00	15	1 day
	1999 Complete Set (12) McDonalds Teenie Beanie Babies TBB MIP	$11.00	12	1 day
📷	O S I T O The Mexican Beanie Babies(12 Available) Is In Mint Condition NEW!	$5.10	12	1 day

You have your own deck of cards, and the winner of each game can take some of your cards to keep. It's like playing with marbles years ago; winners get to keep some of the losers' stuff. The cards provide different abilities and game options, so different decks and different cards can increase your chances of winning. The clever distributors of this game release new cards on a regular basis with some cards in smaller quantities, therefore rarer, than others. All the cards can be played, and to be a good player, you need certain cards, which leads to demand, which leads to trading, and speculating, and investing. Magic cards and related memorabilia are bought and sold every day online.

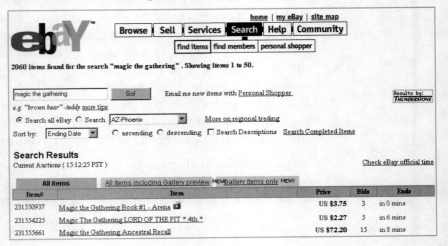

Sports Memorabilia Sure, sports collectibles have always been popular, but there was a real surge of interest in sports cards a few years back. There used to be five card shops in every town and a plethora of card companies producing baseball, football, basketball, and hockey cards—as well as plaques, photos, and commemorative this-and-thats. Interest began to wane when investors realized that most cards did not go up in value and some even went down (to paraphrase the Franklin Mint television commercials). Collector cards are a particularly risky investment, because many cards have no intrinsic value. Unlike a Beanie Baby or Magic cards or Pokémon cards, which can be played with as toys, a sports card often has value only if the market decides it has value. Although there has been a decline in sports collectibles speculation, there is still plenty of online action.

✓1-Click	MARK MCGWIRE ROOKIE CSA10=PSA 10 GRADED GEM MINT DONRUSS #46 CARD@WOW@	$300.00	0	0 days, 00:03:02
	CURTIS ENIS ROOKIE CARD	$3.00	0	0 days, 00:11:01
	JIM EVERETT ROOKIE CARD!!	$1.00	0	0 days, 00:11:02
✓1-Click	📷 MARK MCGWIRE ROOKIE USC SMOKEY RP@LOOK@SCARCE	$9.95	0	0 days, 00:15:17
✓1-Click	📷 10%Off 1st Bidder MARK MCGWIRE ALL-STAR ROOKIE @LOOK@	$9.95	0	0 days, 00:15:18
✓1-Click	📷 MARK MCGWIRE ROOKIE USC SMOKEY RP@LOOK@SCARCE	$9.95	0	0 days, 00:22:06
✓1-Click	📷 1987 TOPPS MARK MCGUIRE ROOKIE YEAR +SHARP MCGUIRE CLASSIC CARD	$11.95	0	0 days, 00:22:06

New Issue Comic Books A little before investors began speculating on sports cards and memorabilia, a similar phenomenon occurred in the world of comics. While a faithful fan of the X-Men (the Marvel Comics superhero group) would always be there to buy each new issue, demand for certain new and innovative titles increased to the point that an issue might not be available after the first day of release. Demand led to an increase in value on even some brand new, mass-published titles to the point that many comic buyers were buying multiple copies of every new comic book in the hopes that they would rapidly increase in value and could be resold within a few months or a year for a quick and pleasant profit. The problem, of course, was that although certain specific new releases were extremely popular and were in great demand, the majority of comic books were worth only the cover price (if that)—especially when everyone and his brother was buying multiple copies. Some issues of popular titles were selling millions of copies. Everyone was speculating, everyone was investing, and hardly anyone was buying comic books to read. Teenagers, college students, and older investors soon ran out of money. The market has settled down a bit since then. A quick look on eBay will tell us that some titles are still speculated on. In sheer numbers of listings, comic books are hard to beat online, and they attract bids from all ages. As a *hot* collectible, interest has moved from newer comics (the kind that attracted speculators) to older, rarer comics in top condition, which have held their value.

		mint spawn and x-men lot !wow!no reserve!	$4.00	-	01/20 11:51
	🎥	📷	AVENGELYNE ACE EDITION # 14 *ACETATE COVER*	$6.50	-	01/20 11:49
			WOLVERINE 1/2 WIZARD EXCLUSIVE	$0.99	-	01/20 11:46
	🎥	📷	GROO THE WANDERER #1 MARVEL EPIC COMICS!	$6.00	-	01/23 11:44
	🎥	📷	GROO THE WANDERER SPECIAL #1! ECLIPSE COMICS!	$15.00	-	01/23 11:41
	🎥	📷	GROO THE WANDERER #6!!! DC COMICS!!	$7.00	-	01/23 11:40
🏠	🎥	📷	LOT OF TEN X-MEN VOL. 1 NO.1 COMICS	$12.00	-	01/20 11:37
	🎥	📷	GEN 13 #0!! FIRST PRINT! FROM IMAGE COMICS	$4.00	-	01/23 11:37
	🎥	📷	Little Paw #3 in Fine condition, furry book	$5.00	1	01/23 11:31
	🎥	📷	EVIL ERNIE SPECIAL LIMITED EDITION #1!!	$30.00	-	01/23 11:26
	🎥	📷	DEATHMATE BLACK!! FIRST PRINTING!	$10.00	-	01/23 11:24
			JLA (current) 1-12Mint BV$90 HOT COMICS!!!!	$0.99	-	01/20 11:23
	🎥	📷	THE DEMON #44!! FROM DC COMICS!	$6.00	-	01/23 11:21
	🎥	📷	THE DEMON #43!! FROM DC COMICS!	$8.00	-	01/23 11:19
	🎥	📷	COVEN #1 FAN APPRECIATION EDITION!!	$5.00	-	01/23 11:16
	🎥	📷	COVEN #1 "JAM" COVER!!! FROM THE MINI SERIES!	$7.00	-	01/23 11:10
	🎥	📷	THE DEMON #45!! FROM DC COMICS!	$6.00	-	01/23 11:08
	🎥	📷	MARVEL ONSLAUGHT EPILOGUE through BOOK SIX	$20.00	-	01/23 11:04

These areas are just some examples of collectibles that are currently in production, and some are not particularly old. Items still in production have no true scarcity, in the same way that antiques, vintage cars, and one-of-a-kind items do. Even if an item is produced in limited quantities, the manufacturer can create a brand new similar item and it can become the latest hot, limited edition. Some items have a *perceived* scarcity, however, and certainly have a *perceived* value. As long as demand is there, prices can and do rise quickly. The problem is you never know which items will go up and which will go down (or stay the same, which in a profit game is almost as bad) and whether interest will be stable enough to allow enough time to buy, wait for an increase, and sell. Prices don't actually need to increase for one to make a profit, of course. You could find an underpriced item in one market segment and sell it for profit in another market, but the principle is the same.

Risks of Speculating Online

Beware of the risks when speculating online. If you are interested in buying collectibles online in order to resell, follow these guidelines to increase your chances of success:

◆ Only buy items in your field of expertise. If you know quite a bit about the Beanie Baby market and have gotten good at predicting which Beanies will be in demand in the months to come, then go for it, find an undervalued new release, buy in bulk, and quickly turn those Babies around for a profit. Do not, however, assume you can do the same with the new quarters honoring the 50 U.S. states. Let the coin experts speculate in that market.

◆ When many different auctions are selling the same items, go for quality. High grade, nice condition items are easier to resell to collectors and will go more quickly.

◆ Know where you will sell before you buy. Don't assume that you will find buyers unless you know they exist. In addition to confirming a viable market online, see if your local store is willing to buy comics from you or if you can sell your Magic cards through the mail.

◆ When in doubt, don't speculate. Try just a couple of purchases until you have learned to be successful. Go slow and build to larger ticket bids. This is a conservative approach, and you may miss out on the chance of a lifetime—but more likely you will save your money, not lose it, and live to play again some other day.

When Spelling Counts

A friend of mine (and the author of a great introductory eBay book) tells a tale of finding a valuable item on eBay and being able to immediately turn around and sell it on eBay for a profit. The secret was that he was lucky enough to capitalize on his and the seller's poor spelling. He was searching for auctions selling older books with illustrations by a certain artist that he loved. This artist had a particularly tough last name to spell. My friend accidentally mistyped the artist's name as a search term. He quickly realized his mistake, but he was surprised to see that a hit came up. A valuable book was listed, but the seller had inadvertently misspelled the artist's name in the title in the same way my friend did. Consequently no one searching for this artist had found the listing, no one had bid, and my friend won the auction for the very low minimum bid. Why not try this trick with your own searches? Look for a Mark McGuire rookie card instead of a Mark McGwire rookie card and see if you get lucky. Also consider alternative spellings (for example, *colour* for *color*, *collectable* for *collectible*).

4 Checking Out the Seller

There are several ways to determine if a seller is trustworthy. Feedback, of course, is the easiest and can be extremely informative. Also, you may trust someone because you have bought from her in the past and have never had any problems. An advanced strategy in judging potential sellers is through analysis of their listings. Let's look at all three methods.

N O T E Many online auction sellers have their own Web sites or homepages and will direct you there in their listings. By all means, check them out. You can learn a lot about someone by seeing what his home looks like (metaphorically speaking).

Feedback

Amazon, Yahoo!, and eBay all provide systems where users—buyers and sellers—can leave positive or negative feedback. The systems (based on eBay's original and, for the time, innovative process) are similar and provide both a number reflecting satisfaction level and written comments about transactions. In the world of scientific evaluation this is called *quantitative* and *qualitative research*. The number can provide a good summary, but it doesn't provide nearly as much depth of information as reading the comments themselves. Perhaps the single best way to learn about not only sellers, but about customer service—the feelings and expectations of buyers, and how to handle trouble or concerns—is by reading through the feedback of sellers and buyers.

Leaving feedback on some of the sites (Amazon is particularly difficult) can be a little laborious, but eBay provides a very easy and efficient way to leave comments about any transaction. You can also keep track of your recent, successfully completed auctions through the Feedback Forum:

1. Choose the Services menu from the top of any eBay page.

2. Choose Feedback Forum submenu.

3. Click the Use Feedback Forum link, or scroll to the bottom of the page.

4. Click Leave Feedback About An eBay User to see all pending comments.

5. Enter your User ID information.

6. Immediately bookmark the page that is created. It lists all recent transactions for which you have not left feedback, and it allows you to leave comments from this central location.

Table 4.1 shows the scoring systems and ins and outs of feedback for the Big Three.

Learning from Experience

Clearly, in the old-fashioned, face-to-face business world if you had good experiences with a merchant you learned to trust them. Online auctions are no different, and here is a list of characteristics of those past encounters to consider:

Was the item as promised?   Was it the correct item, of course, and was the condition as described? Is their "very good" the same as your "very good"? If an item is described as MIB (mint in original box), it should be mint, not BIB (beat-up in original box).

TABLE 4.1 User Feedback Scoring Systems for eBay, Yahoo!, and Amazon

Site	Quantitative Data	Qualitative Data	Collection Method
eBay	+1 Positive 0 Neutral −1 Negative Feedback is shown as a running total next to User ID. Only feedback by unique users is counted.	Comments may be left by either the seller or the buyer and must be tied to a transaction.	Pages allow any user to view feedback. The auction listing and notification e-mail provides links. It is easiest to use your personalized Feedback Forum page, which tracks who you've left feedback for and who you haven't.
Yahoo!	+1 Excellent +1 Good 0 Average −1 Poor −1 Bad Feedback is shown as a running total next to User ID. Only feedback by unique users is counted.	Comments may be left only by sellers and winning bidders. Happy and sad faces summarize the written comments. The original rater may return at a later time and change the rating.	At the close of an auction, winning bidders and sellers are sent an e-mail, which includes a link to the Feedback page. Yahoo!'s My Auction pages also provide links. Users are allowed to modify their feedback scores at a later date.
Amazon	1 to 5 scale, with 1 as the worst and 5 as the best. Number shown is a running average. Multiple feedback by the same user will have a multiple effect on rating.	Comments may be left by anyone who has successfully bought or sold an item. There is no option for responding to feedback left by someone else.	Amazon's Your Account page provides feedback links next to transactions.

Was the seller pleasant?   Life is too short to mess around with unfriendly types. Did the e-mail and any communication that was included in the package sound like it came from a friend? Though your seller need not be your best friend, you'd like for them to be friendly.

Did the seller leave positive feedback?   Just as a satisfied buyer can reward the seller with nice feedback, a satisfied seller should do the same.

Did notification e-mail and responses arrive quickly?   I like instant gratification, and I like to know that I'll get my item as quickly as possible.

Was the package sent quickly?   As soon as my check clears, the package should be sent. None of this "four to six weeks" stuff you see on infomercials.

Was the item packaged securely?   This is probably the best indicator of professionalism and, perhaps, the most appreciated aspect of customer service.

Listing Analysis

When you walk into a store, you probably make dozens of judgments about the quality of the storekeeper from just looking around at the physical surroundings. Perhaps you've even left a restaurant without sitting down because you just got a "bad feeling" that dining there would not be pleasant. Experienced online auction bidders develop a similar sixth sense and can develop "good" or "bad" feelings from just reading through the listing of an item. Of course, it is hard to evaluate the accuracy of intuitive feelings, but experienced users will tell you that they look at a long list of seemingly insignificant details when judging the quality of a seller. Let's look at the elements of a listing that gave me the heebie-jeebies.

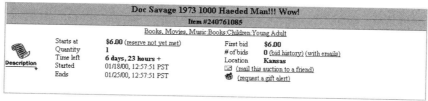

The seller of the item might well be a nice and trustworthy businessperson, worth my time to deal with, but there are several details here that gave me pause:

- ◆ A typo or misspelling in the title. It says "haeded" not "headed." Whoever heard of a "thousand haeded man?" (As opposed to thousand-headed men that we hear about all the time!) I know that anyone can make mistakes, but if a seller is sloppy about typing in the name of the product they are selling and doesn't have the time to proofread for errors, I wonder what other areas of customer service might be sloppy. By itself, a misspelled word has little meaning, and as with the searching for misspelled words strategy discussed earlier, misspellings can help you to buy a treasure for less. My point here isn't that people who make mistakes are bad people and should be avoided. It's just a small detail that can be used in addition to other data you get from your analysis. Just yesterday, I saw a listing description composed of a single 12-word sentence that contained no punctuation and had literally four misspelled words. Strangely enough, the item had no bids. Go figure!

◆ Use of too many exclamation points, *wows*, and other persuasive words in the title. Sellers think these tricks add excitement to the listing and help attract browsers to look at the item or even convince an undecided buyer to bid. To experienced buyers the overuse of these sorts of inducements are so common that they are ignored, at best, or a turn-off, at worst. A few such words can be a powerful inducement to take a look, and in the selling sections we'll discuss that strategy, but when you are a buyer, fight the urge!

◆ The category choice. Tons of Doc Savage books are sold on eBay, but most are not in the category of Books: Children: Young Adult. A seller who does list Doc Savage in this category either has not sold many of these items before (which indicates inexperience) or thinks only young adults should read these literary masterpieces, which a middle-aged man like me finds insulting. (In case you think I am easily offended, I should admit that I am really only mildly insulted.) Regardless of the reason, I start to feel a little concern about the dealer. There is nothing wrong with inexperience, everyone must start somewhere, but a smart new seller would search for similar items already for sale to find the right category. I hesitate to deal with a seller who hasn't given much thought to this process. Knowing which category to pick reflects the experience of the seller with that particular type of item and is, therefore, indicative of the seller's ability to accurately describe the item. If the item is listed in the wrong category, it may also be described incorrectly or rated or valued as better than it really is. This isn't to say that a seller might not intentionally list an item in a related category where it might not normally be in hopes of attracting a new population of bidders, but I sense that was not the case here.

◆ The auction includes a *reserve price* on the item—while similar items rarely have a reserve This is an inexpensive item that likely will sell for a couple bucks. If the seller wants to guarantee that it won't sell for less than that, setting the starting minimum bid at $2 would take care of that. For an inexpensive paperback, having a reserve at all, let alone both a high starting price and a reserve price, is a little silly. The seller gains nothing by having a reserve price. In fact, eBay charges the seller for using the reserve option and will refund that money only if the item sells. Like some of the other complaints on this list, it doesn't really hurt me as a buyer that the seller has made this strange decision, but it does make me worry that if I enter into a transaction with this seller, I might also be entering into the Twilight Zone.

◆ The starting bid is too high. I don't mean it is more than I can afford (which, of course, is the best reason to just keep on browsing); I mean it is unreasonably high. The *starting* bid is higher than the item is *worth*. An unreasonably high price means the seller doesn't know the market, has unreasonable expectations, or might not really want to sell the item. It also could mean that the seller is unscrupulous and is trying to fool inexperienced buyers. A dandy Doc Savage book like the one described in the following graphic sells for about $3 in used bookstores. So what is this seller up to?

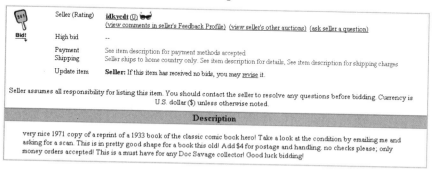

◆ The seller has a 0 feedback rating. This either means the seller is brand new or hasn't generated any positive feedback. The best of the sellers on online auctions began with 0 feedback ratings, so that by itself isn't a red flag. On eBay, a 0 feedback rating combined with the sunglasses icon (which indicates that the seller created a new User ID in the last 30 days) means that the seller likely is brand new. Check the seller's transaction history (by clicking on the 0) to make sure there isn't a bad history here with negative comments canceling out any positive comments.

◆ The item description has errors indicating that the seller isn't the expert he pretends to be. For example, Doc Savage was not a comic book hero, he was a pulp hero. Comic books, as we know them today, didn't exist in 1933, the year of the original publication, which is reprinted in the edition offered here. I don't demand that sellers know everything about the item they are selling, but if they pretend to know a lot with phrases like "the classic…hero" and "a must for any Doc Savage collector," then I am disappointed when they reveal themselves as less than a kindred spirit. On the other hand, perhaps I should take advantage of their ignorance and look for a bargain.

◆ No picture is provided for an item where a picture would be useful or when most of the other items in the category have pictures. The seller asks customers to e-mail him for a scanned image. A good seller will provide all the information I need to make a purchase, and I don't want to go through the trouble of e-mailing, asking for a scan, waiting, and then trying to open it on my computer. It should be a part of the listing right there on eBay.

◆ Information on the condition is fuzzy. This book is "very nice" and "in pretty good shape," but I must "take a look at the condition" by e-mailing and asking for a scan. This is worse than no information. I have no idea what condition this item is in. I smell more risk than I am willing to take.

◆ Postage and handling is too high. Four dollars is more than the book itself is worth. Actual mailing cost for this light-weight paperback book would be about $2.50 total (padded mailer plus U.S. postage).

◆ No checks accepted. It is easier on the customer (and probably less expensive) to send a check than to get a money order. The extra hassle of paying with something other than a check may not be worth it for you.

WARNING   A Certificate of Authenticity is not a *guarantee* of authenticity. Any seller with a computer printer can print one up in seconds, so an item with such a certificate may be no more likely to be authentic than a similar item without a certificate. Know your hobby well, and learn what areas have a high percentage of fraud. Some experts, for example, believe that the majority of autographed sports memorabilia, whether they have Certificates of Authenticity or not, are not genuine.

Advice from the Big Three

On the pages of eBay, Yahoo!, and Amazon, you will find recommendations on how to deal with the issue of trust between buyer and seller and ways to make the buying experience a happy one. Here are their suggestions:

eBay   Tips collected from experienced buyers include knowing a lot about the item you bid on, using feedback and reading the actual comments to check the reputation of the seller, and checking with the Better Business Bureau at www.BBBonline.org. eBay also recommends that you keep detailed records of the listing information and consider calling the seller on the phone to minimize any concerns.

Yahoo!   A Question And Answer page, which lists inquiries from other bidders about the item, is attached to every auction. Yahoo! suggests that you ask for contact information on the Question And Answers page. Sellers' e-mail addresses are harder to find on Yahoo!, but they may be listed on sellers' About Me or Profile pages, which many Yahoo! users create.

Amazon   The ratings next to sellers' nicknames provide information about reliability and promptness. Clicking the sellers' names brings up their entire selling and buying histories. Amazon also suggests that cautious buyers use an escrow service. The best guarantee from Amazon comes through the Amazon A-to-z Guarantee.

Amazon's Guarantee

Unique among the Big Three, and a pretty interesting experiment on their part, is Amazon's emphasis on what they call the A-to-z Guarantee. A buyer of any auction item with a listing that includes the A-to-z Guarantee logo may be covered for the cost of any disputed item. These guidelines (and a few others) apply:

◆ A buyer is covered when a seller does not deliver the item or sends an item which is "materially different" from the description in the listing. An example of a "material difference" is if an item is described as new but is actually used. Amazon makes the final judgment of whether an item is materially different than described.

◆ You must make a claim through a submission form on the site between 30 and 60 days after the close of the auction.

◆ You must be a resident of the Unites States, the United Kingdom, or Germany.

◆ Coverage is up to $250 (higher if you used Amazon's payment service).

The fine folks at Amazon believe that the vast majority of all transactions on their site are between nice, friendly, and honest people and provide this guarantee as a business strategy to encourage those who are fearful of Internet transactions to use their site.

eBay's SafeHarbor

SafeHarbor is both a site on eBay and an eBay concept that transactions should occur in a safe environment. eBay automatically provides Safe-Harbor Insurance for transactions, through the services of Lloyd's of London, the same company known for insuring unusual collections and celebrity body parts. Here are some of the conditions of the guarantee:

◆ Both the buyer and the seller have non-negative feedback ratings.

◆ The item can legally be sold on eBay and is within the posted eBay guidelines.

◆ The winning bid must be more than $25 (because a $25 deductible is applied to all claims) and can be up to $200.

◆ Buyers can file only one claim per month, and it must be filed within 30 days of the end of an auction.

WARNING The 30-day limit on eBay's guarantee and the 60-day limit on Amazon's may sound like plenty of time to file a claim, but that time can pass quickly. With the give-and-take communication between seller and buyer that occurs during a transaction, it may be almost a month before you even know there is a serious problem.

◆ Money must have been sent, in good faith, to the seller.

◆ The seller committed fraud or the item received is significantly different than described.

Be warned that claims are processed in the same way as real-life insurance claims and by an outside company, so reimbursement may take more time than under Amazon's guarantee. eBay says that they pay approved claims within 45 days.

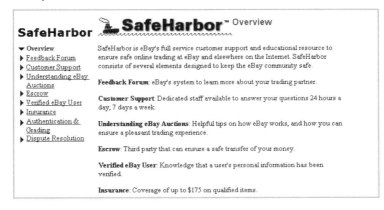

Bidding to Win

Here we will talk more specifically about the game strategies associated with buying. Essentially, if you think of bidding in an auction as a game, you have two possible, winning objectives:

1. Win the auction—at any cost!

2. Win the auction for as low a bid as possible.

Simply having the highest bid as your goal is one thing. Theoretically, that is an easy goal to reach, though one does need to have a source of infinite wealth. (Details, details!) The second objective is a more practical one because, after all, what you really want is to get the item at a good price. This section suggests some tactics for meeting this objective.

5   What Is It Worth?

The *worth* of an item depends on whether you are buying as an investment or because you want the item to keep. If you are buying the item to keep, the worth of the item is based on the lowest price you can buy it for and how much you want it for yourself. If you are buying the item as an investment, the worth is the amount of money you will sell it for. Let's discuss how to determine the value of an item if you plan to keep it.

N O T E   There *is* a difference between the *highest bidder* and the *smartest bidder*. The highest bidder has the largest bid and is committed to purchasing the item. A smart bidder never bids more than the item is worth to him. Sometimes the smart bidder is the highest bidder, sometimes not.

Buying to Keep

The two factors to consider when buying an item to add to your collection are how much you want an item and the lowest price for which you can attain it. To determine how much you want an item, review the steps in number 1, "Budgeting when Buying." To determine the lowest price for which you can attain an item, consider these suggestions:

- ◆ Before searching for an item online, decide how much the condition of the item matters. If you want a book because you want to read it, then it is probably acceptable to you as long as it is in one piece. On the other hand, if you want the book to display it, you want it as nice as possible. Condition determines price in most cases, and you can get it cheaper if you don't mind nicks and scratches (or blueberry pie filling on the edge of every page).

- ◆ Find out how much similar items go for on your auction site of choice. So many sellers are online that on any given day you probably will find similar items successfully auctioned off at one price or another. Take note of those selling prices. Are you willing to pay that much? If not, you may need to look to more traditional outlets for your collectibles. However, auction sites tend to have lower sale prices than typical retail prices—which is one reason for their popularity among buyers—so you may have trouble finding your Holy Grail for less elsewhere.

- ◆ Find out what items cost in retail stores. This simple step is sometimes skipped, and you often sees brand new items online, and even used items, selling for more than they cost at the local department store.

- ◆ Search closed auctions for realized prices—auctions in progress do not give an accurate picture of true sale price.

- ◆ If you have the time and the tools, try *sniping*. (See number 6, "Sniping—Going, Going, Gotcha!")

Buying to Resell

The value of an item you plan to resell is, in some ways, easier to estimate than the value of an item you want to keep for yourself. Collectors must rely on fuzzy, introspective psychology and decide for themselves if "I really, really, REALLY, want that…I'll pay anything!" For the speculator, determining value is a more cold and calculated decision. Guessing what an item will go for in the future is usually based on two forecasting tools: the seller's past experience of what the market will bear using knowledge of trends in the seller's area of expertise and *price guides*.

It is very difficult to consistently predict which contemporary collectibles will quickly increase in value. Even professionals who make their living buying and selling trendy collectibles frequently guess wrong, which makes the business an adventurous one. It is even harder for a part-time business person—the hybrid of collector and investor who characterizes so many of eBay's, Amazon's, and Yahoo!'s auction customers—to guess right frequently enough to ensure a profitable future. To succeed at short-term speculation in the collecting market, you should have a few characteristics that will give you an advantage in the marketplace. You must have enough experience to recognize hot commodities just a bit before everyone else does, you need to have access to a ready market of buyers who compete for what you are offering, and you need to buy low enough that miscalculations in predictions of future profits can be off by a mile without financial devastation. If you have these skills, then online auctions present a great arena to test yourself.

More and more of the great traditional auction houses are developing online auction sites. eBay presents the "Great Collections" site, which is a collaboration with some of these auction houses, at least one of which eBay now owns outright! You can see that there is quality stuff available for the serious investor.

Check out the Appendix for tons of different online auction sites and their Web addresses!

Price Guides

Price guides have become the bibles of many areas of collecting. Although a large book store can provide guides for just about any type of collectible, they are most heavily relied upon in sports card collecting, comic book collecting, advertising premiums, books, and Beanie Babies. Some price guides are remarkable reference works (the annual *Overstreet Comic Book Price Guide*, for example, is a massive, deeply researched listing of just about every comic ever published), although there are caveats in using price guides as the final word on values. Here are some tips to consider about price guides:

◆ Read the introductory material of the guide. What claims do they make about the values they list? Are they based on actual retail sales, auction sales (which may be lower or higher than typical sales), anecdotal claims of the author or other dealers, or wholesale prices? Is the data source specifically described, or is it vaguely referenced with some phrase like "based on the author's vast experience" or "best judgment"? The better price guides will use actual, retail sale prices that have been reported to them or have been found through research. In some cases, the author is a large enough dealer to know what prices they have actually received for merchandise. An actual reported sale price is the best evidence of general values. An average of many reported sale prices is even better.

◆ Be suspicious of guides that list values for a variety of conditions for each collectible they list without explanations for how those values are derived. Often a formula is used to estimate the relative value of an item in a variety of conditions. For example, the reported sale of a turn-of-the-century Bavarian cuckoo clock in great condition for $3,200 is real evidence. By contrast, applying a general rule that says clocks in poor condition sell for 50 percent less than clocks in great condition and listing a Bavarian clock in poor condition as worth only $1,600 may be misleading, and even flat out wrong, if no Bavarian cuckoo clock in poor condition has sold at all. In most collectible fields, price guides use a standard formula for filling in the blanks based on sales values for items that did sell in a particular condition. If your guide does that, it should provide the formula.

◆ How sellers use price guides to determine selling price varies depending on geographic location. In the United States, price guides often are used only as just that—guides—and asking price will be something less than listed values. In Europe, the selling price is more frequently the listed value. (This is why you may get higher bids from overseas bidders for your collectibles.)

◆ The larger price guides also have a habit of guessing values to fill in for gaps in the record. With the millions of different sports cards, comic books, magazines, toys, etc., no guide could possibly receive sales information for everything they list. Yet values are listed for everything. What can they be based on, except some generalized formula blindly applied across the board? It makes you wonder how meaningful these guesses are.

◆ Use your price guide to learn how to grade your collectibles. Most good guides provide detailed information on what the various terms for different conditions (Good, Very Good, Fine, Mint, etc.) mean and how to judge the condition of a collectible. Read and practice the suggested guidelines.

◆ Use your price guide as a reference work to check on the completeness of an item. Are those the correct shoes for the Barbie outfit?

◆ In the fields where price guides are used to set prices, they can be a great guide as to what prices your future customer will expect to see. Items bought substantially "below guide" can be more easily sold at a profit. Keep in mind, though, that most collectibles on online auction sites sell at below guide—some substantially so. This is true except for the hottest of the hot new collectibles, which are too new to have achieved a stable market. Most of those sales are going to speculators who expect prices to rise even higher.

◆ How old is your price guide? Quality guides are updated at least every year. Some collectible markets fluctuate so rapidly that you may need a monthly update, not just an annual report. Check to see what guide and which volume your favorite dealer is using. That's probably the one you should use, too.

◆ Although the guides may be updated every year, not all the information is. It is good to see what local dealers are using for their guide. For example, some catalogs change editors and publishers, which causes problems with their pricing.

NOTE Use all the information at your disposal to determine a good selling price before you bid, including department store catalogs, trade publications, retail stores, and local antique shops. It is sadly all too common to see bids online for items that are easily available at much lower prices in the real world.

Some price guides are available on the Internet, though they seldom provide free access. Guide publishers make their money through the sales of the guides, so it is hard to get reliable value information on a Web site. Table 5.1 gives just a flavor of what is available.

TABLE 5.1 Selected Online Price Guides

Item	URL
Autographs	www.collectors.com/price.html
Antiques	www.kovels.com
Beanie Babies	www.beanietown-usa.com
Coins	www.collectors.com/price.html
Hallmark Ornaments	www.msdatabase.com
Hot Wheels Cars	www.alleyguide.com
Precious Moments	www.msdatabase.com
Records	www.collectors.com/price.html
Sports Collectibles	www.beckett.com/priceguides
Star Wars Figures	www.galstar.com/~mrmiller

6 Sniping—Going, Going, Gotcha!

Oh, the stories we can all share! Stories about the first time. For me, the first time was back in the crazy 1990s and I was fairly new to eBay. Some poor fool had offered for auction an original Charles Schulz drawing of Snoopy on his doghouse fighting the Red Baron! This, surely, was incredibly valuable and a sure, solid gold investment for the future—not to mention really cool to own. The minimum bid was reasonable, but—here's the amazing part—no one else had bid! Were they crazy, these other eBayers? My excitement mounting, I entered a bid, I set my maximum bid at two bidding intervals over his minimum to scare off any other would-be bidders. Ha! Clever, no? As fate would have it, I was entertaining in my palatial estate during the closing minutes of the auction. (Okay, that part is made up. I *was* hosting a party, but my parties are seldom entertaining.) I rudely excused myself to run downstairs to my computer to watch the closing seconds of the auction. My bid sat as the only bid—with only 5 minutes left. I wondered if I would need to insure the drawing—only 4 minutes 22 seconds. I'd never actually purchased insurance for a collectible before—3 minutes 42 seconds. I wondered if insurance companies rely on price guides to determine value? They probably did—the stupid saps. I chuckled to myself. Huh? I'd been outbid! Someone came out of nowhere and suddenly chose this last minute to bid on *my* drawing! They must have just stumbled across it and decided to bid. Just my luck!

Confidently, I entered a new maximum bid $100 higher. Aha! Success. Now I had the highest bid—1 minute 22 seconds. I got Snoopy on my wall. Drawn by Charles Schulz himself—55 seconds. I'm glad I had the wisdom to watch these last few minutes. Who'd have thought anyone would bid at the last minute? eBay's maximum bid system bids for you automatically by proxy, so there's no benefit to waiting to the last minute, I thought—39 seconds. Refresh. 23 seconds…17 seconds…Wait! No! Noooo! I've been outbid again! Unbelievable! Furiously, I typed. My fingers flew. But, of course, it was too late. I'd lost it.

How to Snipe

I lost the Snoopy drawing. Good thing, too, because the price had gone much higher than I ever wanted to pay. The drawing had been mine for a full week, and I lost it at the last second. Someone had been lurking, watching the auction and waiting until the last possible second to bid. They had done this to lock out the possibility of any competing bids. I realized, as I returned to what should have been my victory party, that I had been sniped. *Sniping* is the auction word for what those other bidders did to me, but there is no word to describe how much wiser I felt. On that day I first realized that there was some strategy to this eBay game.

For bidders with any experience at all, it doesn't take long to learn about sniping, read about it on discussion boards, see debates on auction community sites, and get sniped themselves. It happens so frequently, especially now with the proliferation of bidding software, that the odds are good that you have been sniped. If so, you know the feeling. For a couple of years, I've taught an online course that is an introduction to eBay. The students share their experiences with the rest of the class as they bid for the first time at auction. A good percentage of them, on their *first* time out, lose to snipers. Their descriptions of how they feel range from good-natured ("They wanted it more than I did") to feelings of having been actually violated! It would be hard to overestimate the negativity of such an experience for some folks.

Of course, as a behavior, waiting until the last minute to bid for the first time isn't immoral, unethical, or even *mean*. It certainly feels that way to the second highest bidder, though—which explains why it is the number one complaint you hear from bidders. Yahoo! and Amazon have wisely responded to these concerns and have auction formats available that eliminate the possibility of sniping. This is easily done, by simply continuing an auction until no more bids have come in for a few minutes. There is no "last second" anymore, so there are no "last second bids." In the meantime, until they change things on eBay (and you must think they will), should you learn to snipe, so that at least you will be on an equal playing field? If you have the time, organization, or the software, you should consider it. Keep in mind that you still want to calculate your best bid, and make that bid. But suppose you want to make that bid just as an auction is ending? Here's how:

1. Locate an auction item you'd like to bid on.

2. Mark that auction listing so that you can go straight there in your browser. You can make it a bookmark. You can also mark it online as an auction you would like to follow. This will place it on your one-stop personalized auction listings page, which is available under various names on the Big Three sites (e.g., My eBay page). The bookmark method guarantees the quickest trip.

3. Write down—on a *real* piece of paper—the auction (using the name you used for your bookmark) and the time it ends. You might find it easier to simply print the auction page and use that for your record keeping. Be sure to write down the ending time using your local time! The online sites featured in this book all use Pacific time as their official times, so you may have to do a little math to figure out your local closing time.

4. Keep your auction listings in order by when they end.

5. Keep track of the time. (Yahoo! even offers a countdown ticker for each auction that you can keep open on your computer desktop. Just click the *countdown ticker* next to an auction's ending time.)

6. About 15 minutes before an auction is scheduled to end, fire up your browser and go directly to the auction of interest. This gives you enough time to deal with the occasional technical delays that may occur.

7. Once you are on your auction's page, verify that there are a few minutes left, and check the current high bid. Is it below your *magic number,* the maximum amount you previously decided you would bid. (Need I emphasize the *previously*? Don't let the emotions of seeing a higher bid cloud your perception of how much an item is worth to you!)

8. If you decide to bid, continue to watch the auction until about a minute is left. You must continuously refresh your screen during this time, to watch the time countdown, and to watch for any changes in the high bid.

9. With 60 seconds or so left to bid, begin the steps necessary to enter a bid. Enter the exact bid you decided upon, provide the identifying information you need (if you have previously *signed in,* as you can on

all three sites, you will save time here), and then let your cursor hover over the final submit button. With about 30 seconds left to go, make you bid. This should allow enough time to compensate for delays due to traffic, modems, and the like—which could slow up the registration of your bid. You know your own speeds and equipment better than I do, so feel free to adjust the timing to match your comfort level.

10. When the page comes up registering your bid, everything should all be over, one way or the other. You may have won or lost. Other snipers may have been shooting at the same target you were. It was almost a game of chance to see who could record the win.

Snipe Hunting with Auction Trakker

The CD that comes with this book includes sniping software so you can be the hunter rather than the prey. Now, there's no need to worry that those sneaky other bidders (you know the ones I mean) will wait until the last second to bid and steal something cool out from under your nose because you can be one of those other bidders! Among the dandy software included on the CD is Auction Trakker, your new sniping partner and "bestest pal!"

WARNING Sniping software works only until your auction site updates or modifies its bidding pages. Whenever you can, you should verify that your automated bids really registered. You don't want to miss an item because your software was out-of-date. As changes at the site are made, your software provider likely will provide a free update.

You should fully explore all the tools included on the CD because they do an amazing number of different things. I'll only highlight a few of them throughout this book. For example, here's how to use Auction Trakker to snipe for you on eBay:

1. At eBay, find an auction you'd like to bid on. Copy the auction number.

2. In Auction Trakker, choose Add Auction from the Actions menu.

3. Paste the auction number into the Add Auction window.

4. Click Snipe Setup. Choose how early before the close of the auction you would like to dial in, log on, and bid. Choose the snipe amount. Click Save Snipe.

5. Leave your computer on and walk away. It's that simple!

In this example, you can see two auctions stored and set up for sniping. I also have a window open showing the auction on eBay for which I have entered a snipe amount.

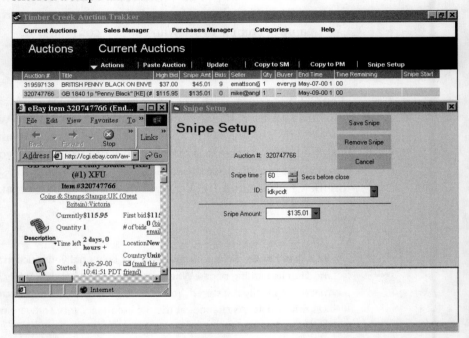

NOTE All the software included with this book is updated and improved often. Be sure to check for updates when you first use your software!

The software provided in this book makes sniping easy, and it is hard to think of any reason why a bidder with sniping software shouldn't use it as long as it is up-to-date. Sniping with software has advantages over not sniping at all. If you bid by hand, however, without the aid of sniping software, the question of whether to snipe or not is a bit more complicated.

Table 6.1 presents some advantages and disadvantages of sniping over not sniping at all when you must do all the work yourself.

NOTE Friends who live in different parts of the world who want to snipe by hand can use each other to bid on their behalf if their time zone makes last second bidding more convenient. Of course, you must trust that your friends will pay for any items you win for them.

TABLE 6.1   Sniping by Hand: Advantages and Disadvantages

Disadvantages	Advantages
Sniping without software (watching the final seconds of an auction and responding rapidly) encourages you to bid more than you should. Earlier in this book, we talked about how to decide what your maximum bid should be. Seeing what others have bid is not a component of that decision-making process. Some, however, may get caught up in the excitement of the auction action and jump in when they shouldn't. Are you one of those people?	Bidding at the last second decreases the chance that a competing bidder will be able to respond in time by increasing his maximum bid.
Manual sniping can force you to sit in front of your computer at times when you would rather be elsewhere.	Waiting until near the end of an auction to bid hides the fact that there is any interest in the item and discourages other bidders. Some bidders browse through miles of listings and only notice auctions that have received bids.
Sniping requires that you keep track of when an auction is ending, log on during the last few minutes, check the winning bid, and enter a higher bid. That's a lot of work and if you snooze, you lose.	Waiting until the end of an auction to bids allows more time for research, comparison shopping, and hard core ruminating about how much to bid and whether to bid at all.

7 Don't Bite into the Bad Apples

All three of the big auction sites warn you that while the huge majority of sellers on their sites are good folks, there are a few bad apples. Here are some, mostly common sense, ways to avoid them:

◆ Use the feedback ratings. Don't totally rely on the rating (and on all sites the bigger the better), but also read a sampling of comments.

◆ Make sure a high rating was due primarily to the user selling items, not just buying items. Users earn points for both, and just because a person is a good buyer to deal with does not mean they will be a good seller.

◆ Be wary of a seller who uses the same photo to represent different items or who doesn't use a photo of the actual item that is being offered. No two stamps are alike, so the seller shouldn't show a scan from a Scott's catalog of what the stamp looks like. The seller should show a scan of the stamp she is actually selling.

◆ Read the item description carefully to get a feel for the seller's knowledge and trustworthiness. See number 4, "Checking Out the Seller," for a particularly obsessive-compulsive analysis of an item listing.

◆ Consider paying by credit card, if you can do so responsibly. This will speed up delivery and give you consumer rights to challenge a charge. It is easier to get money back from a credit card transaction than from a payment by check or money order. Also, there is a $50 liability on credit card charges that you do not authorize, so if you notify your credit card issuer the moment you know something is wrong, you can lose $50 at the most. This makes credit card use even safer (in some ways) than paying by check. There are risks associated with sending credit card information over the Internet, but I believe the benefits outweigh the risks. You decide what risks you are comfortable with.

◆ When buying with a credit card, look for users with secure sites. To get secure servers, retailers must provide a lot of information about themselves, increasing the likelihood that they are legitimate.

◆ Be cautious of sending payment to a post office box. It is more difficult to track down the seller who does not have a street address.

◆ Avoid sending cash. If it is a very small amount, I suppose you could take the risk, but it is a dangerous proposition with large sums of money.

◆ If you do bite into a bad apple, by all means pursue the site-specific remedies available. On Amazon and eBay, see if you are covered by their "insurance" guarantees and file the paperwork on time. The fraud reporting form at eBay, for example, is simple to fill out. As you see, the site walks you through the process step-by-step. If there are avenues through the legal system, pursue them, too. You will help others, not just yourself.

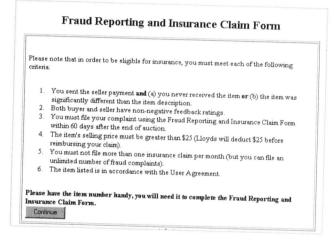

Fraud Reporting and Insurance Claim Form

Please note that in order to be eligible for insurance, you must meet each of the following criteria:

1. You sent the seller payment **and** (a) you never received the item **or** (b) the item was significantly different than the item description.
2. Both buyer and seller have non-negative feedback ratings.
3. You must file your complaint using the Fraud Reporting and Insurance Claim Form within 60 days after the end of auction.
4. The item's selling price must be greater than $25 (Lloyds will deduct $25 before reimbursing your claim).
5. You must not file more than one insurance claim per month (but you can file an unlimited number of fraud complaints).
6. The item listed is in accordance with the User Agreement.

Please have the item number handy, you will need it to complete the Fraud Reporting and Insurance Claim Form.

[Continue]

Shill Bidding

Online auction users may have to contend with two forms of unscrupulous bidding. One form hurts buyers, another hurts sellers. We'll talk about how buyers can be harmed here. We'll look at how sellers can be hurt by the practice later.

Both of these bidding tactics can be grouped under the term *shill bidding*. A *shill* is a decoy. In the confidence game lingo, a shill is someone who pretends to be a customer in order to affect or persuade the real customer or target of a con.

To con a buyer, shill bidding works this way:

1. After an auction is underway and (usually) after a bid has already been made, the seller places a bid on his own item. The seller either does this himself (using a separate User ID to avoid detection) or through a shill, someone else working with him.

2. If the first (real) bidder has entered a proxy bid amount that is higher or equal to the shill bid, the first bidder's bid is automatically increased. Even if the shill bid doesn't act to increase the first bidder's bid, it places the bid higher for other interested buyers who may come along and want to bid.

3. If the auction ends with the shill bidder as the high bidder, the seller pays the auction site their cut of the selling price, but doesn't actually sell the item to anyone.

When this form of shill bidding fails, the seller is only out a small amount of money. When it succeeds, it increases the winning bid unfairly, and the seller can make quite a lot of ill-gotten profit. Shill bidding violates the Big Three auction site policies and, moreover, it could be construed as fraud under United States federal or state laws.

Because this sort of shill bidding undermines trust in the community of online auction users, the sites indicate that they are developing methods of identifying and removing offenders. For example, eBay describes a "shill bidding detection tool" that they use to analyze bidding patterns across listings. Presumably, it looks at the identities of sellers and bidders to identify consistent pairings of sellers with the same non-winning bidders. These sites also have more information about the true names and addresses of sellers than users have, so detection should be easier for them than for us. As a bidder, how can you spot a shill bidder? It isn't easy. One thing you can do is to examine the recent completed auctions of a seller and look at the bidding history. Does the same person bid in many of the seller's auctions. Check that bidder's own auctions. Does your seller show up as a bidder in his auctions? Again, of course, you can also check feedback comments. Has he been accused of shill bidding in the past? When shill bidding strikes against a seller, as we'll see later in the book, you can spot it; but as a buyer, you need good detective work to notice anything afoot. Does the seller have retracted bids in his history? Shills helping each other as sellers can bid a huge amount on an auction to find out what the real bidder's maximum bid is, retract the bid, and then re-bid just enough for the real bidders bid to reach the maximum. (By the way, some sites prevent re-bids in the same auction when someone has retracted a bid to prevent this sort of mischief.) As with other negative aspects of online auctions discussed in this book, it is a rarity, but shill bidding is a threat to the hard-earned trust built up in the online auction community—which is why the sites have placed a priority on detection.

8 Completing the Purchase

Amazon, Yahoo!, and eBay all send notification e-mails to the seller and winning bidder letting them know that an auction has ended and giving the results. Soon after receiving it, you, the buyer, should receive an e-mail from the seller congratulating you on your fine play and reminding you about what you agreed to pay—the winning bid plus the additional postage and handling costs. Some sellers will offer additional protection in terms of insurance or delivery options for an additional charge.

The important point here is that no dealer should require a fee that was not described in the item description. Some listings say "postage is additional," but they do not report the actual price they will charge. This may be because they want to charge the actual mailing charge to where you are, which is a sign of good customer service.

WARNING   Do not feel you must accept any cost or charge that was not described in the item listing! This is similar to the $300 protective undercoating that I was asked to pay for when I thought I had negotiated a final sale price on my last car.

The dealer now provides a mailing address. If all is as it should be:

1. Reply to the seller's e-mail with a big "Thanks! The money is on it's way!" Provide the seller with your mailing address so they can prepare the packaging.

2. Send the money.

It's as simple as that. How long should it be before you get your Star Trek Blooper Video or your Confederate Lined Infantry Button (whatever that is)? It depends on how you paid and where you sent it.

◆ If you paid by credit card, it should arrive 7 days after authorization..

◆ If you paid by money order, it should arrive in 14 days.

◆ If you paid by check, it should arrive in 21 days.

◆ If you live in, or are mailing to, a country other than the United States or Canada, as many as three weeks or more could be added. The world is still a pretty big place.

These estimates may seem pretty short compared to traditional mail-order purchases, which promise 4–6 weeks for delivery. The special nature of Internet transactions demands a higher quality of customer service. Once the money is in the seller's hand, the item should be sent immediately.

If the item does not arrive in a reasonable period of time, you should e-mail the seller asking what the status of the transaction is. Be polite, and give them the benefit of the doubt. In almost all cases, two e-mails—one confirming agreement to pay and one asking for status—are the only two direct communications with the seller that will be required. To be nice, you can also send an e-mail letting the seller know that you received the item and will enter positive feedback on the auction site. In worst case scenarios, however, a series of other communications may be necessary. Here is a step-by-step process that should be followed, in most cases, until the item you won is received:

1. Receive notice from the site that you won an auction.

2. Send an e-mail to the seller confirming your understanding that you won the auction and that the money will be sent. Provide your name and address.

3. Let the seller know when the item arrives. This is all that you will ever have to send with the large majority of your auction purchases, and the process will stop here.

4. If the item does not arrive on time, send a follow-up e-mail asking if payment was received and if the item has been sent.

5. Allow another week for delivery, and then send one more "request for status" e-mail.

6. If there is no satisfactory response, send an e-mail indicating your dissatisfaction at how things are going and that you plan to seek remedy under the site's guidelines.

7. Answer any e-mails from the seller in a polite manner until the issue is resolved or the item arrives. After your complaint e-mail, you have no obligation to contact the seller again. Situations differ, however, so use your judgment on whether there are legitimate reasons for delays, but don't allow yourself to be pushed around.

9 Expert Bidding Advice

For this book, I rounded up a panel of Internet auction gurus—real people like you who have been successful as both buyers and sellers—and asked them to share advice on a variety of online auction strategies. All three have positive feedback, but my goal wasn't to talk to the super-buyers or super-sellers online—although one member of the panel does have a particularly impressive record. For these advice sections, I wanted comments from normal, bright, fairly typical users. People like you and me who have given some thought and analysis to the right ways to do things. Here are their thoughts on the fine art of playing a winning bid.

User ID: xjhawkx
Category: Sports Cards

"I deal mostly with sports cards and condition is everything. And since everyone seems to have their own ideas on how to grade a card, I will only bid on cards that have been professionally graded or those with pictures and detailed descriptions. If they do not fall into one of these categories, I pass

them by. The second point about bidding that is extremely useful to me is I have to tell myself that there will always be another card just like the one I want sometime in the future. I do not HAVE TO HAVE this card. And lastly, I like to look at those bids that are just ending and do some sniping. This works very well with auctions that end during odd times of day like after midnight and before 6 A.M."

User ID: aaagh!
Category: Comic Book Art

"Only bid at the very last moment if you have a take-it-or-leave-it attitude; otherwise, bid as much as you are willing to pay—it won't make much difference. You can almost always save money by bidding in the last 10 seconds of an auction, but remember to account for Internet delays—you could try to bid $50 for something, only to find your bid didn't get through and the item sold to someone else for $3.

If a seller constantly sells items you are interested in, bookmark their auction page and check back to it regularly.

Typos mean bargains—try alternative spellings of words, like The Simsons instead of The Simpsons. Rare collectibles can be had for a tenth of their normal price just because the seller misspelled the name, and the auction is 'invisible' to anyone looking for it"

User ID: ssabellico
Category: Star Wars

"If I am interested in an item, I note when the auction ends. I check back on that day religiously and place my bids accordingly"

Expert Summary

Did you notice that our experts don't all agree about some things (bid up front or wait until the last minute)? However, they have thought about how they like to operate and the reasons for or against their choices. That is the defining characteristic of advanced online auction users.

Buying into the
Online
Community

Here we'll discuss the role of the buyer as a member of a community. eBay, Yahoo!, and Amazon are all designed to create a friendly, cooperative environment where "townspeople" work and play together. There are chat rooms, community bulletin boards, and even magazines dedicated to communication between members of these virtual towns.

As a contributing citizen of a virtual community, the buyer has both opportunities and obligations to leave the community a better place than she found it. Here's how.

10 Let 'Em Know What You Think

One of the really great innovations of the Internet auctions is the ability to leave feedback. Alerting other users to the strengths and weaknesses and overall "goodness" of sellers and buyers really helps to shape the online auction community. It is a sound psychological principle—in a society, behaviors that are rewarded increase and behaviors that get a negative response decrease in frequency. For a community like eBay, Yahoo!, or Amazon, the principle should work just as well.

Comments left by users are stored where they can be reviewed by others who might want to buy from or sell to other users. The nature of the feedback (positive or negative) is converted into a number and added to the user's feedback rating. If the feedback was good, the number increases; if the feedback was bad, the number decreases. On eBay and Yahoo!, the number of good comments are added together and the number of bad comments are subtracted from that total. On Amazon, the ratings are assigned (by the person leaving the feedback) a value from 1 to 5, with 5 being the best. These values are then averaged over all transactions. Amazon also lists the total number of transactions, which resulted in this average. Glance back at number 4, "Checking Out the Seller," to compare feedback systems. Here is eBay's feedback page:

Leave Feedback about an eBay User

Your User ID:
You can also use your email address.

Your Password:
Forgot your password?

Are you tired of typing in your User ID and Password over and over again?
Save time by signing in. (You may also sign in securely).

idkycdt
User ID of person who you are commenting on

Item number (please include since all feedback must be transactional)

Is your comment positive, negative, or neutral?
◉ positive   ○ negative   ○ neutral

You are responsible for your own words.

Your comments will be attributed with your name and the date. eBay cannot take responsibility for the comments you post here, and you should be careful about making comments that could be libelous or slanderous. To be safe, make only factual, emotionless comments. Contact your attorney if you have any doubts. **You will not be able to retract or edit Feedback you left.** eBay does not remove Feedback unless there is an exceptional circumstance. Think before you leave Feedback.

N O T E   On eBay and Yahoo!, the higher the feedback rating, the more transactions the user has been involved in. This rating, then, can work as a measure of experience. On Amazon, however, a very high rating is possible without a long history of transactions, so be sure to use both the rating and the number of transactions to judge the quality of an Amazon user.

Leaving feedback is voluntary. Under what circumstances should a buyer leave feedback? There is a diversity of opinions about what a buyer's obligations are to leave feedback about a seller after a successful transaction. I feel a little bit like a film critic who is about to pan a film that all the other critics like, because my own opinion is at odds with the majority. In fairness, I'll present the feelings of most online users up front and remind you that this is what most people have decided, so you should certainly give it the weight it is due. However, I won't pass up this opportunity to share my own thoughts—even if they don't have the support of the masses.

The majority view is that because the online auction world depends on constant feedback to evaluate the quality of sellers, it is essential that buyers leave positive or at least neutral feedback at the conclusion of any transaction that has gone smoothly. This tells the online world that there is one more satis-fied customer. As the number of satisfied customers grows, so does the seller's feedback rating. The comments and ratings then provide a trust-worthy and valid measure of the seller and allow buyers to choose good sellers and avoid bad sellers. It is a remarkably clever and, generally speaking, accurate system for buyers to rely on. Because sellers depend on good feedback, many feel that buyers have a social obligation to leave posi-tive feedback every time, unless the experience is negative. Almost all would agree that buyers should leave negative feedback after a transaction that is not completed to the buyer's satisfaction. Those who feel that buyers have an obligation to routinely leave feedback after routine transactions argue that this is a good way for buyers to contribute to the community.

My opinion is that the obligation an Internet auction buyer has to the com-munity of other users is limited to leaving feedback whenever a transaction is negative and when a transaction goes *unusually* well. Under this philos-ophy, routine purchases would not result in feedback. As I've said, this is not a commonly held opinion, by any means. Certainly sellers, especially new sellers, appreciate as much positive feedback and comments as they can get because this rapidly increases their ratings and improves their rep-utation, which results in more and higher bids and more sales. Because of this, many sellers include in their notification e-mail a request for feedback if you were satisfied. I would argue, though, that it should require more than satisfaction to motivate a buyer to leave feedback.

The analogy that guides my thinking on this issue is that of a customer writing a letter to a business. In the old days, before e-mail and the Internet, only two things would motivate a customer to take the time and energy to send a letter after a transaction. The customer was either unhappy or unusually happy after better than expected service. Service of expected quality would not result in feedback one way or the other, simply because good service was expected. A winning bidder should expect a smooth and pleasant transaction and not be so taken aback when it hap-pens that they rattle off positive feedback. I expect professional service from the professionals who sell on eBay, Yahoo!, and Amazon. If they go beyond the call of duty, I am quick to reward them, but have they earned a reward if they only engage in the expected minimal customer service? They do have my money, after all, and maybe that should be reward enough. On the other hand, successful sellers at online auction sites point out that the Internet is very different than a storefront business and reputation is more important. Without feedback from buyers, reputations cannot be built and truly good, high-quality sellers cannot be identified.

Another consideration when developing your own personal feedback policy is whether there is ever a reason to leave neutral feedback. The sites allow you to indicate if feedback or the transaction was positive, negative, or neutral. Neutral feedback, though, isn't really feedback at all, and one wonders about the value of leaving a neutral comment. The exception might be on Amazon, where a comment attached to a rating of 3 out of 5 could serve to raise a low rating or lower a high rating. Those who hold the view that leaving feedback after every transaction is a social obligation suggest that the neutral category be reserved for transactions that eventually ended up OK, but the transaction had some bumps along the way.

Examples of Yahoo! and Amazon feedback charts are shown here and provide quick snapshots of a seller's quality. The Amazon seller (who I don't know, and I hope they don't mind the free publicity) has particularly impressive numbers.

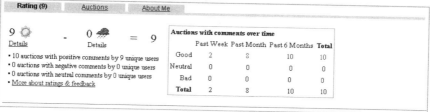

But What Should I Say?

Table 10.1 lists some real comments left as feedback. Some are positive, some are negative, and they cover a variety of situations. They should be useful as suggestions of what words to use in feedback. There isn't much room in a feedback window and a little art is involved in choosing just the right words. The examples shown here are from Amazon, but they could be from any of the sites, as certain phrases have become popular (for example, "Would buy from again"). One rule to follow when leaving negative feedback is to state only the facts and not make a personal attack. "He is a fraud!" is not appropriate; "I never received my merchandise!" is better. Be as personal as you want, though, when leaving positive feedback (for example, "What a great guy!")

TABLE 10.1 Examples of Strong Feedback Phrases

Positive	Fast efficient delivery. Smooth and quick transaction. Highly recommend! It looked great! Thanks!! Great packaging. Would definitely bid again! Great experience. I have them bookmarked! As beautiful as the picture! Exactly as described; even better condition. KEEP UP THE GREAT SERVICE Good communication A+++++++++
Negative	Auction is marked "will ship to other countries" but they won't. I did not receive all of my shipment and was treated very rudely. This vendor will not e-mail me back so I cannot pay! Extremely poor communication. I did not receive the item I won. The advertised boxcar was 6-26215, I was sent 6-26230. Be careful.

What is interesting about the real comments shown here is that they were all about the same seller. On Amazon, the dealer's overall rating was 4.7 out of 5, so there were many more positive comments than negative, but I certainly got a more complete picture of the seller than I would have by just looking at the rating.

What should be included in the feedback you leave? As a buyer, you want to tell other buyers about the transaction in ways that will be helpful to them in deciding to buy from this seller or to avoid them. Specific components of feedback that buyers find useful include:

◆ Comments about the friendliness of the seller and the transaction.

◆ Descriptions of the quality of packaging.

◆ Indications of the speed of delivery.

◆ Descriptions of the quality of merchandise. This is particularly important for buyers of non-collectibles who are often looking for items comparable to new or retail condition in quality.

◆ Would you buy from them again?

When leaving negative comments, here are some guidelines to keep in mind:

◆ Describe the specific behavior resulting in negative feedback.

◆ Avoid criticizing a seller's character. All you can be sure of is his behavior during your transaction. (This is one way to avoid any potentially libelous comments, as well!)

◆ Describe as objectively and unemotionally as you can what your complaint is.

◆ Avoid exclamation points. Online comments, whether in e-mail, chatrooms, or on bulletin boards are often misinterpreted, and emotional indicators like exclamation points frequently have their impact greatly exaggerated.

What happens if *you* get negative feedback and you take issue with it? Yahoo! and eBay allow responses to feedback to be included in your permanent record. (I wish my high school principal had a similar policy!) If you feel that the feedback creates a misperception or is an outright lie and want to state your position, attaching your side of the story to the damaging feedback couldn't hurt. Though you may have every right to respond defensively and rattle off some negative feedback of your own, be sure to choose your words carefully. Keep your comments accurate in describing the situation, and show regret for any authentic misunderstanding. Your image to others in the online community may come out intact and might even improve. I know my respect often increases for a buyer or seller who handles a complaint well. Another possibility is that by showing restraint now, you may actually regain a positive relationship with the user who left the feedback in the first place. Remember that, on Yahoo!, users can go back and change previous ratings they left in the past.

WARNING As a buyer, do not leave positive feedback until you have actually received your purchase. Perhaps it is obvious that you shouldn't praise a seller until you have completed the transaction, but it happens.

NOTE Leaving feedback on Amazon can be tricky. If you are involved in a successful auction, the e-mail you receive will have a link for feedback, or you can find it through your Auctions You've Won or Auction Items Sold page, linked on your Your Account page. After choosing an overall rating (5 is excellent, 1 is awful) and leaving a comment, push the Submit button. You must submit before leaving the page or the feedback is not recorded.

eBay's Feedback Forum

If you routinely leave feedback, you can respond to all your transactions with the ultra-spiffy super-convenient Feedback Forum page on eBay. You get to this do-all page by choosing Services and Feedback Forum from eBay's always present top-of-the-page menu. By providing your User ID and password, you create a list of all the transactions in the last 60 days for which you have not left feedback. On this single page you can enter feedback, mark whether it is negative, neutral, or positive and post it for hundreds of transactions with one click of the Leave Comment button. Shown here is an example of a page of recent purchases with comments about to be left. The page shows both purchases and sales.

User ID	Item#	Item		Ended
vegallery@aol.com	275774769	POOH PIGLET TIGGER & EEYORE ANIMATION ART		Mar-11-00 13:39:29 PST

Is your comment positive, negative or neutral?
(• positive (negative (neutral (Don't leave feedback now

Great item. Sent quickly and packaged securely!

Your comment (max. 80 characters)

| oh2collect@aol.com | 274398828 | JONATHAN WINTERS AS MAUDIE FRICKERT CEL RARE! | | Mar-12-00 15:40:17 PST |

Is your comment positive, negative or neutral?
(• positive (negative (neutral (Don't leave feedback now

A swell cell Thanks for the quick mailing and your selection of unusual items!

Your comment (max. 80 characters)

| gadmark | 276730631 | Quest of the Spider 1933 Doc Savage Hardback | | Mar-12-00 16:06:42 PST |

Is your comment positive, negative or neutral?
(positive (negative (neutral (• Don't leave feedback now

11 Keeping Track of Your Auctions

If you are like most auction users, it won't be long before you buy more than just an occasional item. Soon, you may well be bidding and winning so rapidly that you'll start to forget where you got that *RARE RUSSIAN FT2 PANORAMIC CAMERA BOXED* or that *MADONNA AND CHILD OLDMASTER PAINTING.* You'll probably lose track of the advertised condition of the item and whether it came with a certificate of authenticity and a variety of other bits of information that it would be nice to know.

Some good record keeping would be useful here. If you are more than an occasional bidder and especially if you are a hardcore buyer, I recommend a simple record keeping system. Purchase a three-ring binder and a three-hole punch (which combined can be had for less than $20), or if you do most things on computer (and I'm guessing Sybex readers do) set up a spreadsheet or database file. Much of the stuff you will want to save is most easily stored as hard copy, however. Keep the following information:

- ◆ A printout of the item listing page at the conclusion of every auction you win. This is crucial because if any problems with the seller occur and last more than a few weeks, the original listing may no longer exist on the auction site's server.

- ◆ A copy of the confirming e-mail that the seller sends. You can discard this when the item comes and you are satisfied. (If you want to save a tree, you might be comfortable just keeping this e-mail on your computer and forgo a hard copy.)

- ◆ Any certificates of authenticity or similar written claims of an item's characteristics and any written guarantees. (The three holes you make along the side of these items won't hurt anything.)

- ◆ A ledger that has a row for each item, costs, claims, and other information. This can be on paper or stored as a spreadsheet. The paper copy is often more convenient and certainly more portable.

Ledger Domain

Your record-keeping ledger should be a one-stop archive of what you bought and who you bought it from. You can use it to search for good sellers who provide good service and the stuff you need. It will also be useful when it comes time to resell; you will know your profit or loss and how you are doing as an investor. Table 11.1 shows an example of a ledger, but you may find other categories of information that are useful for you to keep track of.

TABLE 11.1 A Useful Ledger of Purchases

Item/ Item Number	Seller's ID	Winning Bid P & H Total Cost	Date/ Notes
Autographed Joe Montana Plaque eBay 246476331	Sfandkc	$55.01 $4.00 $59.01	1/12/01 Cert. of Authenticity
19th-Century Crosscut Saw Yahoo! 14966322	pbunyan23	$17.50 $3.50 $21.00	1/14/01

TABLE 11.1 A Useful Ledger of Purchases (Continued)

Item/ Item Number	Seller's ID	Winning Bid P & H Total Cost	Date/ Notes
Popeye Pez Amazon 0124L254136	Olyvoilcollector	$72.00 $2.50 $74.50	2/11/01

As you develop a list of trustworthy sellers, you can expand your dealings with them by visiting their Web sites, asking about catalogs, and potentially developing a trading relationship. The ledger can also be invaluable for looking back at the decisions you have made over the months and years and evaluating your performance.

 Auction management programs, like the ones included on the CD you got with this book, can retrieve and store much of this information for you automatically. They will also print your records for you whenever you would prefer to have a hard copy.

12 Learning from Sellers

If you are a collector and you win a well-run auction, you really win in two ways. First, you get something you want at or below the price you want to pay. Second, you learn a little more about your hobby. A wealth of information about whatever you collect is available from reading listings on eBay, Yahoo!, or Amazon. Additionally, you can learn about customer service and pricing for that day when you become a seller.

Learning about Your Hobby

By browsing through the long listings in your category of choice and reading the item descriptions, you can learn a ton. Potential nuggets of information include:

◆ Names of the major players in your field. These might be the popularly collected artists, writers, producers, actors, designers, athletes, builders, manufacturers, or advertisers. You'll find out who and what is "in."

◆ The items or variations of items that exist. I never knew that Doc Savage pulps were reprinted in Canada in the 1940s and 1950s, but there they were—up for auction!

◆ The jargon of the field. What abbreviations are used? What terms are used to describe the condition of your collectibles?

◆ The aspects of an item collectors feel are important in determining worth. All those Beanie Baby listings tell me that the tag is still attached, so I know that is important to collectors.

Table 12.1 translates a few of the abbreviations you'll run into while perusing auctions lists.

TABLE 12.1 Common Terms Found in Listings

Abbreviation	What It Means
BU	Built-up. As in a model that's been put together. Also, "Brilliant, used" in coin collecting (and when describing your brain at the end of the day.)
F	In fine condition
G	In good condition.
HTF	Hard to find.
MIB	Mint in box. The term "box" is often used loosely to describe the original container even if it isn't a rectangle.
Mint	Now almost universally used in all collectible categories to indicate a pristine, "like new," unused-looking condition.
MIOJ	Made in occupied Japan. Used primarily by glass, porcelain, figurine, and similar item collectors.
MOMC	Mint on mint card. Describes a variety of products manufactured and shrink-wrapped onto a piece of cardboard.

TABLE 12.1 Common Terms Found in Listings (Continued)

Abbreviation	What It Means
MWMT	Mint with mint tag. One of the myriad of phrases which have mystical meaning to the collectors of Beanie Babies.
NM	Near mint
NR	No reserve. Theoretically, it advertises the fact that the seller is willing to sell for whatever the market will bear. Sometimes, though, a NR auction will have a high minimum bid, so " no reserve" doesn't guarantee a low opening bid.
OOP	Out of print. Originally referred to books only, but now applied to movies, cards, etc.
VF	Very fine condition.
VG	Very good condition.

Learning How to Be a Seller

We've already talked about ways you can judge the quality of a seller (see number 4, "Checking Out the Seller," number 7, "Don't Bite into the Bad Apples," and number 10, "Let 'Em Know What You Think"). Buying is a great way to learn about listing techniques, communication skills, and customer service. Pay attention to your subjective experience as a buyer. What made you feel good about a listing, auction, or transaction? What made you feel less than good? Here are some aspects of your experience that you might learn from:

◆ Words in the title of the auction. If you found the auction through a search, did the inclusion of a key word help? Was a year included in the title, or a color? If you found the auction by browsing a category, what was it about the title that caught your eye? Did the listing say anything more than just mention the particular type of item you were looking for?

◆ What was the quality of the item description? Did you have all the information you needed to make a decision?

◆ Additional charges. How much additional postage would have turned you off?

◆ Photos. Did the presence or absence of a photo of the item affect your bidding decision?

◆ Seller rating. Did you check the rating? Did you read comments? How did the rating affect your confidence in the seller?

◆ Reserve auctions. Did the presence of a hidden reserve price affect your attitude toward the process?

◆ Communication. Did reading the seller's e-mails make you more or less confident in the seller?

◆ Packaging. How did the quality of the packaging affect your feelings about the whole process?

Power Selling Starts Here

The first part of this book concentrated on the experiences of the bidder and buyer on Internet auctions. As you read that section, I hope you were processing the ideas through your mind not just as a buyer, but also as a seller. The rest of *Online Auctions! I Didn't Know You Could Do That...* concentrates on the strategies of power selling, but we will always refer back to the strategies and concepts discussed in the buying section.

We have already looked at budgeting, costs, and checking out other users from the perspective of the buyer. Now, we will look at those issues from your perspective as a seller.

13 Budgeting when Selling

When you run an auction, your budgeting issues center around the costs of that auction, whether to set a high minimum bid, what price to set for the bid, whether to set a reserve price, and for what amount to set it, and the amount of any additional fees, such as postage and packaging. The next section covers the costs of using eBay, Yahoo!, or Amazon to run the auction itself, and number 16, "Figuring Profit from All the Angles," covers different pricing options. So let's look at the most basic budgeting concern— How much do I charge?—and develop some strategies.

Sellers in traditional markets follow a comparatively simple process to determine the asking price for a product. Economic formulas can suggest the exact price that will maximize volume and profit. If a price is too high, demand will drop, but sales may still be large enough for a good net profit to occur. Lowering the price will increase demand, but perhaps not enough to offset the drop in per-item profits. Business plans are research and data driven. What does the consumer expect to pay? Is quality associated with price? What does the competition charge? What are the costs of production, employees, and wholesale buying? Over time, as sales and experience build, a traditional retail business accumulates a wealth of data to estimate the results of different asking prices. You might expect me to say something like "and selling at auction is no different." Well, selling at auction is *very* different.

Internet auction selling differs from traditional selling and its strategies for determining the asking price in several ways:

◆ The seller doesn't pick the asking price, the buyer does. While you, as the seller, have control over the least you will sell for, the auction process itself determines the final asking price. It may be at the minimum bid you set, or it may be far above that. It is pretty exhilarating when you offer something that you picked up for pennies and don't know much about and watch as the high bid unexpectedly grows tremendously.

◆ For most auctions, an increased number of customers (bidders) increases the price, but not the number of sales. This is the opposite of traditional selling, where an increase in customers increases sales. The exception is any auction using the Dutch auction format, where duplicates of the same item are sold though a single listing.

◆ If only one bidder is interested in an item, then you sell for peanuts. If two bidders are greatly interested in the same item, then you sell for big bucks. If you are selling a collectible that you have only one of, you can't sell more than one, but you can sell that one for more. It is an exciting world where attracting just one more customer can skyrocket your profits.

◆ Chance plays a role in the final selling price. If that extra bidder just happened to wander by at the right moment, then it was only luck that made the price increase. The potential customer pool at the online auction sites is getting to be pretty darn massive, though, so luck plays less of a role in the size of the winning bid than it used to play.

◆ The goal is to get as much as you can for an item, not to figure out the best sale price beforehand. Although the traditional strategies of coming up with the right price, trying to increase interest in your item, and advertising to the right market still play a role, the goal of a winning online auction strategy is to increase the size of the single winning bid.

◆ Some internet auctions differ from real-life in-person auctions in one crucial way that affects the final selling price. On eBay, the auction ends at a given time and day. Non-Internet auctions end when there is only one bidder still interested. There are no time limits in the real world, but there often is in the Internet world. This is an artificial restriction created by eBay, and it is the weakness of the system that is the most criticized by experienced sellers. It allows sniping, which bothers bidders, and can keep a selling price lower than actual demand would, which bothers sellers. In response to this concern, Yahoo! and Amazon allow auctions to extend beyond the closing time as long as the bids are still coming in.

NOTE The list comparing auction strategies to traditional pricing strategies applies most accurately to the auction of one-of-a-kind items (where there is, strictly speaking, no competition) and one-item auctions (where there are plenty of them out there, but you have only one to sell). A third auction format—Dutch auctions—follows more traditional pricing strategies. In Dutch auctions, the seller has many copies of the same item and is interested in selling as many as possible at a buyer-determined fair price.

Number 1, "Budgeting when Buying," advises that you should determine how much an item is worth to you in order to know your maximum bid. When you're selling, you don't care how much an item goes for (theoretically), as long as it is above a profit point—that is, as long as you make money. *Profit* is a hard concept to define for those selling collectibles at auction. Consider these possible definitions of *profit* and *winning:*

Profit = Total selling price minus cost   Under this definition, you add up all your expenses—what you paid for the item, the costs of running the auction, the costs of mailing, and, maybe, the cost of your time—and you subtract that amount from the money you receive from the winning bidder. If there's anything left over, you win; if there is a negative amount, you lose.

Profit = The profit you made on this sale minus the profit you would have made by selling elsewhere (through ads, trade shows, retail stores, and so on)   Most people selling online could use more traditional outlets for selling their stuff. Because winning bids often don't match book value, retail value, or even wholesale value, you should be concerned about the lost potential if a winning bid is much lower than you could have gotten elsewhere—even if you made a profit under the first definition.

Profit = Total selling price minus the cost of listing the item and the cost of postage and packaging   This definition does not include what you paid for an item and, at first thought, may seem unreasonable. Under this theory, as long as you earn back a little more than the cost of the transaction, you have won. This attitude is surprisingly common, and it isn't as ridiculous as it appears. You'll learn more about how losing money can be construed as winning in number 20, "Aren't I Supposed to Make a Profit? Maybe…."

Pick your favorite definition of profit. (I'm sure your accountant and loved ones are hoping you will pick the first or second). Under that definition, determine the dollar amount that represents profit. That amount and any-thing higher becomes your "winning bid" as a seller.

14 Hidden Selling Costs

In the first part of this book, I listed all the potential costs I could think of that buyers could potentially be forced to pay in addition to the winning bid amount. They apply here as we discuss selling and what costs to figure into your profit strategies. After we look at these additional cost possibilities, rear-ranged to reflect your perspective as a seller, we'll add to that the price of running auctions at the Big Three. (It turns out, for example, that Yahoo! is free, which immediately puts them in the running for teacher's pet.)

Transferable Costs

Some costs of selling are routinely passed on to the buyer. For example:

Shipping   What are the actual mailing costs for this item? It will depend on where the buyer lives. We discuss these specifics in number 55, "Shipping and Handling Charges."

Packaging   It is reasonable for you to include in your shipping and handling fee the actual cost to you for the packaging materials you use.

Insurance   Many quality sellers offer shipping insurance, at the buyer's expense, to protect the buyer. This is a nice option for the buyer to consider. If your selling policy is that all mailings *must* be insured and the buyer has no choice in the matter, make sure you clearly spell that out in your listing.

Safer and Quicker Shipping   Shipping in the United States using sources other than the regular U.S. Postal Service is a helpful option to make available. However, a seller interested in customer service leaves alternate shipping as an option, not a requirement.

NOTE   I have mixed feelings about the best strategy when it comes to deciding who should pay for insurance and fancy delivery options. The seller's options are to always buy insurance for shipping and require the buyer to pick up the cost, always provide it without charging the buyer, or to offer it as the buyer's option. A similar choice must be made about whether, for example, to always ship UPS, FedEx, or Priority Mail. The question is how either choice affects the buyer's perception of customer service and his willingness to pay. Sellers are free to set any parameters on a sale that they want as long as those parameters are presented up front—just as a shopper is free not to bid if he doesn't like those parameters.

NOTE   Here's a quick tutorial on the U.S. Postal Service, UPS, and FedEx. Using the U.S.P.S. is the easiest, and it has many delivery options. Obtaining pick-up service from FedEx is the easiest. UPS requires a weekly paid account. All of these services offer "proof of delivery" options. FedEx has the best reputation for paying insurance claims quickly.

Questionable Fees

Sometimes sellers ask for additional money from buyers that go beyond what is fair and reasonable. A couple of "don'ts" follow:

Handling   Collecting money for postage is reasonable, but additional costs due to time, employees, storage, and so on are the cost of doing business and should be included when you calculate your profit point. Asking customers to pay more than is necessary irritates them. Small rounding up, like charging $3.50 for shipping and handling, instead of the exact $3.20 that Priority Mail costs, probably won't bother many people.

Listing   I recommend that buyers avoid sellers who require payment of a listing fee. As discussed earlier, you should include the cost of auctioning in your profit planning and adjust your selling price accordingly.

Overhead Costs

There are some costs associated with doing business that are unrelated to the fees you are charged by the auction sites. Take these into account:

Internet Costs   In addition to Internet connection and e-mail costs, do you have a Web site that primarily supports your auction selling activities? If so, figure that as part of the costs involved. If it costs you money whenever you are online, either through direct charges or because you are tying up the office phone, you will appreciate the ability to compose listings offline and upload quickly all at once. As we discussed in the buying section, your time is valuable—especially if you are in the business of selling and your time online is taking you away from that long line of customers at the counter! The applications on this book's CD will help you to save that all too precious time.

Banking Costs   Do you have a business account, with its additional costs? Are you operating through your personal account? Do you accept credit cards? What does it cost you for each transaction? You might consider the credit card processing services offered by all major auction sites. As you can see on Amazon's application form, they ask you to provide lots of information. Provide your checking account number to them, and a pile of money from sales will eventually appear in your account magically (though a somewhat magically smaller pile it will be when Amazon takes their cut).

WARNING Unless you need the capability to accept credit cards only on occasion, don't jump in whole hog and rely on one of the auction services as your primary credit card server. Their fees may well be higher than you would pay to a traditional, dedicated retail service. On the other hand, PayPal at www.paypal.com, along with some other providers independent of the auction sites, is offering nicely competitive fee rates.

Whoops! Even More Costs?

Sometimes things go wrong. When they do, there may be more costs. Consider:

Additional Postage   If you charge a standard fee for postage, it will cost you on those occasions when you miscalculated or have a distant delivery location.

Additional Banking Costs   Your bank probably charges you for submitted checks that bounce. Even your best, most honest customers will make mistakes now and again.

Registered Mailing Costs   You may have to spring for the occasional special delivery letter to try to settle a dispute.

Not-So-Hidden Selling Costs

Earlier we compared the differences between auctions in the real world and auctions on the Internet. In addition to the time limit imposed on Internet auctions, the other major difference is who pays for the auction.

In the real world, the buyer pays for auctions. If you win an auction, you don't pay the winning bid price; you typically pay that price plus some percentage above that price. This additional fee of 10–15 percent pays the auctioneer, the auction house, the cost of advertising, and so on. On the Internet, the seller pays. A fee based on the winning bid is charged to the seller. This is in addition to other fees required for the listing and various auction and listing options. Table 14.1 lists the standard fees for our three auction sites. Table 14.2 lists some optional fees that you may incur. Keep in mind that even the charges on the most expensive site (eBay) are probably less than the overhead you would pay selling in the real world.

NOTE   Remember that the prices discussed here (and anywhere specific costs are mentioned in this book) are accurate only until the sites decide to change their prices. They were accurate at the time of this writing and provide a good method of comparison across sites to get a sense of relative costs when choosing the location of your next auction.

TABLE 14.1 Standard Online Auction Fees

Site	Basic Listing Fee		End of Auction Fee (if item sold)		Reserve Price Auction Fee	
Yahoo!	None		None		None	
eBay	Opening Minimum Bid $0.01–$9.99 $10–$24.99 $25–$49.99 $50 and up	Fee $0.25 $0.50 $1.00 $2.00 Cars, Trucks, and RVs have a $25 listing fee. Real Estate has a $50 listing fee.	Winning Bid $0–$25 $25–$1,000 $1,000+	Fee 5% $1.25 + 2.5% after $25 $25.63 + 1.25% after $1,000	Reserve Price $0.01–$24.99 $25 and up Reserve price auction fees are charged only if the item does not sell.	Fee $0.50 $1.00
Amazon	$0.10 (for now)		Winning Bid $0–$25 $25–$1,000 $1,000+	Fee 5% $1.25 + 2.5% after $25 $25.63 + 1.25% after $1000	None	

NOTE For large winning bids, Amazon and eBay charge an end of auction fee of exactly $25.63 and 1.25% of the amount beyond $1,000. Why the seemingly random $25.63? Well, these giants in the Web world must have pretty sophisticated calculators, because if you take $975 (from the previous pricing level, $1000 – $25) and multiply that by 2.5% and add $1.25, the total equals $25.625, which rounds up to $25.63.

TABLE 14.2   Optional Fees

Site	Fancier Listings	Special Services
Yahoo!	Category Featured $.25 per day You can pay more per day to have your listing featured higher at the top of listings in each category. Whoever pays the most gets their listing the highest, and so on.	Merchant Auction Order Manager $29.95/ month Allows auctioneers to process credit cards through Yahoo!.
eBay	Bold $2 Category Featured $14.95 Home Page Featured $99.95 Gift Icon $1 Gallery $0.25 Gallery Featured $19.95	Buyer Can Pay with Credit Card $0.39 + 3.9% of transactions over $10. Billpoint, eBay's service, will process credit card orders for you.
Amazon	Bold $2 Category Featured $14.95 Home Page Featured $99.95	Buyer Can Pay with Credit Card $0.25 + 2.5% of transaction amount. Amazon will process credit card orders for you.

To summarize all these fees and options:

♦ Yahoo! currently doesn't charge either the seller or the buyer for anything.

♦ Amazon currently charges almost nothing to list an auction.

♦ End of auction fees are identical at eBay and Amazon.

♦ Amazon's fancy listing fees are identical to eBay, while eBay offers additional listing options.

♦ Amazon and Yahoo! offer credit card services for sellers to offer buyers.

♦ Yahoo! and Amazon have a really interesting system for getting your Category Featured listing noticed. With this system you essentially bid against other sellers for good locations. (I'm currently trying to convince my publisher that what's needed is an *I Didn't Know You Could Do That…* book on the strategies in determining for best amount for a seller to bid daily to get the best listing placement on Yahoo! or Amazon. Surely, 600 pages would be enough to solve this brain teaser.)

15 Checking Out the Buyer

You can identify good, trustworthy bidders and customers through posted feedback, past experience, and analysis of their behavior.

Feedback

We've already examined the various feedback systems offered at Yahoo!, Amazon, and eBay. Both numbers and words are left by users to reflect positive or negative trading experiences. On eBay and Yahoo!, big numbers are good. On Amazon, ratings close to 5.0 are best. Judging prospective buyers by reading comments left about them by past sellers is a tougher job. The main difficulty comes from the reality that many sellers have left glowing reviews of buyers in an attempt to get repeat business. Not that there is anything wrong with the practice (in a few chapters, I'm going to recommend that you do the same thing), it just means that praise of buyers should be taken with a grain of salt.

Certainly, superlative feedback comments are flung at sellers, too; but what tends to be missing from the feedback files of buyers are the small complaints that are sometimes left about sellers. This is perfectly natural. If I have won and received an item and feel okay about it, but I wish it had arrived better packaged, I might leave some constructive criticism. Even if I intend to do business with the seller again, there is no harm in leaving the information. If I am a seller, on the other hand, and my customer's check cleared just fine, but it didn't arrive for a couple weeks, I'm not likely to leave feedback with a polite complaint about how long it took the buyer to pay. There's nothing to gain for me, if I hope to sell to the slowpoke again.

Sellers have more to fear from leaving negative feedback about buyers than buyers do from leaving negative feedback about sellers because they can potentially be hurt the most. Customers can respond to posted feedback about themselves in ways that can hurt a business's reputation, or so the paranoia goes. So why make waves, many sellers figure, and they don't leave negative feedback about buyers. Later on, we'll discuss what your feedback policy should be as a seller. For the time being, remember that strong criticisms of buyers are rare, which means that if you do see them, pay particularly close attention.

Here is an example of well-written positive feedback about a buyer. Notice the phrases that convey the quality of the transaction: good communication, A+, good buyer, quick payment, and so on. The sellers are providing a valuable community service and accurate feedback, but the number of comments is really more informative here than the words used. What is most telling in analyzing this particular buyer is the lack of negative feedback. Negative feedback comments about buyers, when they can be found, tend to fall into just two categories:

◆ The buyer didn't send money (which I guess, technically, means they weren't a buyer, but just a bidder).

◆ A seller is responding to negative feedback that a buyer has left about the seller.

Perhaps the most crucial bit of information on eBay's feedback page (in their "ID Card") is the number of retracted bids. For most buyers, this will be zero, if you see many more than that, treat this as a yellow flag to proceed with caution.

NOTE On Amazon, you can leave feedback even if you haven't been involved in a transaction with a user. If someone retracts a bid in your auction and you aren't satisfied with the reasons, leave feedback describing the event.

The feedback systems of all three sites allow you to skim and quickly identify negative comments. By all means, check out the feedback of your winning bidders. You do not have to accept a bid from a buyer you do not trust.

User: mr.mike99 (134) ⭐ **Date:** Sep-20-99 20:13:07 PST	**Item:** 150755933
Praise: Love this guy, he was high bidder in multiple auctions, A++++++++	

User: nodwar (271) ⭐ **Date:** Sep-20-99 19:53:28 PST	**Item:** 150704618
Praise: SUPER FAST PAY!!!!!! Great to work with. Rated AAAAAAAA+++++++++++++	

User: mr.mike99 (134) ⭐ **Date:** Sep-16-99 18:13:15 PST	**Item:** 150744125
Praise: GOOD EBAY BUYER, WON SEVERAL AUCTIONS, A+++++++++	

User: sbergerbhs@aol.com (34) ☆ **Date:** Sep-15-99 05:07:20 PST	**Item:** 153138316
Praise: Responded quickly after auction and paid as promised	

User: ctopjian@aol.com (194) ⭐ **Date:** Sep-12-99 07:45:31 PST	**Item:** 139874954
Praise: Excellant, quick, smooth transaction.	

User: nightlandbooks (168) ⭐ **Date:** Sep-10-99 14:42:15 PST	
Praise: Prompt, smooth transaction! Good communication! Highly recommended!	

User: argosy@iname.com (712) ⭐ **Date:** Aug-24-99 14:11:46 PST	
Praise: Good to deal with. Prompt. Let's do it again. Thanks. RDG	

Past Experience

What makes a good buyer? As you build a base of customers, you will find yourself judging the quality of each buyer. Here are some components of a transaction that indicate a good buyer, the kind you would like to collect:

◆ Rapid response to e-mail. A good customer has easy access to the Internet and checks her e-mail every day. You know you have a gem of a buyer if she writes you first!

◆ The first response includes her real name and a real-world mailing address. This means she is concerned about helping you to begin preparing packaging. It also means she knows that on Web transactions, it is a good idea to prove that she is an honest-to-goodness human being and not a prankster or troublemaker or worse.

◆ He tells you which item he won. You probably have more than one current auction going on and they may all sound similar when described as simply *the beanie baby, the clothes, the book,* and so on.

◆ Money arrives quickly. The benefit of quick payment is that you can complete the transaction quickly.

◆ He notifies you when the package has arrived.

◆ She leaves positive feedback about you. A high feedback rating is the number one way that potential buyers will judge you, and every little bit helps! Because some buyers (like me) don't feel obligated to leave positive feedback routinely, you should nurture the ones who do.

WARNING If you do get e-mail from a bidder saying he has won an auction, be careful to verify that he is the winner! Occasionally, losing bidders will try this ploy to buy an item out from under the nose of a winning bidder. You should report any of these auction interception attempts to the site and to the winning bidder. They are a clear violation of site policies, not to mention illegal.

Selling to Win

This section talks specifically about the strategies associated with selling. The winning objective for each auction is to sell your item for as high a bid as possible. We'll look at:

- ◆ Choosing different auction formats
- ◆ Determining opening and reserve prices
- ◆ Communicating quickly and clearly via e-mail
- ◆ Responding to trouble

16 Figuring Profit from All the Angles

Sellers have some control over what an item will sell for at auction. They can set a *minimum bid,* which is the amount below which they will not sell. On all three auction sites examined in this book, you can protect yourself against selling an item for less than you want to by either of two ways:

Setting a starting bid   In all auctions, the seller decides the amount of money that the first bid will be. Buyers who aren't willing to pay at least this amount cannot take part in the auction. An *opening bid,* a *minimum bid,* and a *starting bid* are all the same thing.

Setting a reserve price   If a seller sets a *reserve price,* the highest bid at the end of the auction is not considered a winning, binding bid unless it is at or above the reserve price. A reserve price must be at or above the starting bid, but it may be much greater than the starting bid. Auctions that use the reserve price option are called *reserve auctions.* The crucial element of reserve auctions is that the reserve price is known only to the seller; it is *hidden* from the bidders.

Because all auctions have a starting bid, you must set a starting bid—you have no choice. The choice is how much to set it for, which is discussed in number 18, "Setting Opening Prices and Reserves." This discussion focuses on the question of using the reserve price option.

As a tactical choice, there are two factors to consider when deciding whether you should use a reserve price or not. The existence of a reserve price will have some effect on the behavior of bidders. Also, the use of a reserve price may affect the cost of listing the auction. Listen up!

How Reserve Prices Affect Bidding Behavior

The Amazon Web site provides a good summary of its position toward reserve auctions and how they affect bidders. Amazon explains why they discourage sellers from setting a reserve price:

- ◆ Bidders "dislike" reserve auctions.

- ◆ Reserve auctions can be "frustrating" to bidders.

- ◆ Unreasonably high reserve prices decrease the likelihood that the auction will end with a winning bid.

The first two items of concern regard bidding behavior, so let's examine them first.

When prospective buyers find an interesting item in a reserve auction, they have no idea what the minimum selling price demanded by the seller actually is. They can't judge whether they agree with the seller about the actual value of the item. Most bidders tire quickly of bidding in auctions they don't win; so unless they think a meeting of the minds between them and the seller is probable, they may just not bid at all. Obviously, with few bidders, the high bid probably won't grow very high.

Bidders also dislike reserve auctions because they often feel they have been mistreated. A low starting bid attracts them to the auction in the first place. They bid some amount they are willing to pay, they are listed as the highest bidder, but they still haven't come close to beating the reserve price. They don't even know if they are close or not. In their minds, they have wasted their time and have just been used by the seller to get the high bid up higher toward the reserve price.

For these reasons, some bidders may avoid reserve auctions. Of course, if you are selling a one-of-a-kind item, you may annoy some bidders with a reserve price, but they will have to bid anyway. The problem with this logic, though, is that many (maybe most) auction purchases are made on impulse, and any hassle or annoyance that interferes with that impulse can't be good for business.

NOTE Reserve auctions can be useful for finding the fair market value of an item when you have no other source of information. Set a high reserve and see how high the bids will go. This method requires many interested bidders, however, to provide a fair test.

NOTE If the theories for successful online auction selling discussed in this book could be boiled down to one idea, it is the theory applied here to reserve auctions. *Many, perhaps most, auction purchases are impulse purchases.* The correct choice for sellers will always be to choose those options that encourage this impulse, and avoid those options that discourage this impulse. Reserve auctions fight against the bidding impulse.

The third argument against reserve auctions presented by Amazon and eBay—Yahoo! doesn't seem to care, but because auctions are free on Yahoo!, why should they care?—is that reserve auctions, especially those with unreasonable reserve prices, will also decrease the chances of a seller selling an item. Certainly, this is true, but experienced eBay and Amazon users suspect a hidden motive for the larger sites to discourage the practice of reserve auctions.

If there is no sale, these auction sites will make money only from the listing and they won't get their cut of the selling price. Because Amazon has very low listing charges as this book is being written, their profit will be made only when an item sells. The higher listing prices on eBay allow them to make some money even if items don't sell, but they certainly appreciate the added profit from successful auctions.

Of course, sites, sellers, and buyers are all happier when auctions are successful, so the position against reserve auctions isn't surprising, and the motive isn't so hidden. However, another *possible* hidden motive is that eBay and Amazon believe they are missing profits due them from sales *off the books.* I suspect that *some* sellers commonly sell through eBay and Amazon without paying them their "fair share" of the sale price. (And it *is* their *fair share,* by the way. When you agree to sell through eBay and Amazon, you agree to give them a cut of any sales directly due to your auction.) Here's how those sellers might do it:

1. A seller starts an auction with an unrealistically high reserve price.

2. The auction ends without a high bid that has met the reserve price. Amazon and eBay record the auction as unsuccessful and charge the seller only for the listing costs.

3. The seller sends an e-mail to the highest (but losing) bidder and says "Gosh, you know, I think I *would* be willing to sell my autographed Alan Ladd Paramount Studios cafeteria receipt for less than my reserve price after all. Do you still want to buy it for your bid amount?"

4. The buyer happily accepts the deal, sends his money, the seller sends the item, and no one is the wiser.

The auction site could be losing a lot of money for big ticket items— and the revenue lost from even small items when there are millions of them can add up, too.

The evidence that Amazon and eBay fear this is implicit in their policies concerning reserve auctions:

◆ Amazon hides the identity of a high bidder in a reserve auction, unless it ends with a winning bid. Unscrupulous sellers don't know who to contact unless the reserve price is met. (Very clever, Amazon!) Often, though, high bidders will e-mail sellers and reveal themselves.

◆ eBay charges an additional fee for reserve auctions that is only collected if the reserve price is *not* met. The only major change in their pricing structure in years came in 1999, when eBay notified users that they opposed reserve auctions so strongly that they would charge for choosing the reserve price option. Two weeks later, presumably because of a boatload of complaints, they revised their new policy to include a refund of this extra listing fee if the item sells. That eBay, whose auction system is rightly regarded as the model for others to emulate, would be willing to tinker with their policies, shows how concerned they are about reserve auctions.

How Reserve Prices Affect Costs

When you're considering reserve auctions, don't forget the additional cost if you are listing on eBay. Keep in mind that prices, of course, are always subject to change. If the reserve price you set is less than $25, you will be charged $0.50. If the reserve price is $25 or above, a dollar will be assessed. This amount is refunded to your account if the auction is completed with a winning bidder. The extent to which this small charge hurts your profit depends on whether you end up with a bid at or above your reserve price. Sellers who consistently sell and don't just produce a long series of interesting, but unsuccessful, listings aren't penalized by this charge. Amazon doesn't charge additional listing costs for reserve auctions. Not yet.

So, to summarize, I think you should have a strong reason before choosing the reserve auction format, especially on eBay, to convince me that it is a good idea. If you believe that setting a low starting bid will get the auction rolling and create some competition that will eventually force the bids up to your reserve price, I'm willing to accept that possibility, but:

◆ The reserve should be reasonable.

◆ You must be pretty sure you are right to counteract all the good reasons against using reserve prices.

17 Auction Wrinkles

We've already talked about two auction formats—standard and reserve—but there are others, as shown in Table 17.1. Here's a handy-dandy table listing the wide variety of auction experiences that await.

Yahoo! really deserves some credit here for being the first to provide both the Buy Price concept (the same as Amazon's Take-It Price auction format) and, most important, the auto-extension auction (part of all Amazon auctions, now), which mimics the excitement and true value-setting accuracy of real-world auctions. eBay should consider the auto-extension system.

TABLE 17.1   Auction Formats

Auction Format	Description	Sites
Standard	The seller sets amount of opening bid. Highest bid wins the auction.	Amazon eBay Yahoo!
Reserve	The seller sets a reserve price. Highest bid at or above the reserve price wins the auction.	Amazon eBay Yahoo!
Dutch	The seller has more than one copy of an item. Bidders say how many they want at their bid price. Any bid at or above the starting price wins the auction. The bidders who bid the most get their items first. All winning bidders are required to pay *only* the lowest winning bid amount per item, even if it is lower than they themselves bid.	Amazon eBay Yahoo!
Private	The identities of the seller and the bidders are hidden. This format is chosen when the item being auctioned is potentially embarrassing, like Doc Savage paperbacks or neon renderings of the Kansas State University wildcat mascot, Power Cat.	Amazon eBay
Buy Price	The seller sets a buy price. If a bidder bids that amount, the auction ends and the bidder wins the auction. This essentially converts the auction into a classified ad.	Yahoo! Amazon
Auto-Extension	In this format, the auction ends when the bidding stops, not at a predetermined time. This is how live real-world auctions have always worked, but it was not part of the original eBay system (and still isn't). Amazon automatically extends any auction by 10 minutes if a bid has been received. Yahoo! allows sellers to choose auto-extension as an option when they create an auction listing.	Yahoo! Amazon
Restricted Access	Sellers and bidders must be adults. This is verified through a credit card on account.	eBay

It would end sniping (a major source of irritation among losing bidders) and simulate the stimulation of the live auction.

Dutch Auctions

The Dutch auction format is a little more complex than other formats, so spending a little time thinking about it would be useful. If you have many copies of an item you are selling, you can list them under a single Dutch auction listing, instead of running many separate auctions. Set a minimum starting bid at which you are willing to sell each duplicate. Because many items are available, bidders indicate both how much they are willing to pay and how many copies they want at that per-item price. They can say they want all of them, just one of them, or any number in between. The amount of the bid acts to prioritize who is first in line to get all the copies they want—in case the total number of items requested is more than is available. The twist, though, is that winning bidders are not required to pay the *highest* bid among them, they only have to pay the *lowest* bid among them.

How bidding works in Dutch auctions is best understood through example. Imagine that you and I are both bidding in a Dutch auction. The seller is offering 50 copies of a new Nintendo video game entitled Princess Meow-Meow 2001. The starting price is $4, so we must both bid at least that amount. I bid $4 and say I want 12 of them. You bid $5 and say you want 20 of them. No one else bids. You win the auction because your bid was highest, and you are first in line to buy your 20 video games. There were more than 20 available, though, so I am among the winners, too. Because the lowest bid among us winners was $4, you don't have to pay $5 a piece for your toys, you only have to pay $4 each. After your 20 are purchased, there are still enough left for me to buy my 12. I, too, pay $4 a piece for them. Sellers who choose the Dutch auction format usually set a starting bid high enough that they will make a profit. The only way that items will sell for more than the starting price is if someone wants to buy so many duplicates that there aren't enough left for any other bidders. In this case, the highest bidder gets the items at the higher bid price.

NOTE An interesting wrinkle in the Dutch bidding rules is that the bidder who asked for the second most items is only required to buy them if his *entire* order is still available after the winning bidder's order is filled.

18 Setting Opening Prices and Reserves

How much do you want for your Napoleon-signed letter about the Italian campaign? The first step in deciding what to set as your starting bid, or as your reserve price, is asking yourself "How much?" We talked a bit about defining *profit* in number 13, "Budgeting when Selling," and we'll discuss selling at a loss in number 20, "Aren't I Supposed to Make a Profit? Maybe...." However, the best way to decide how much you want is to determine the lowest selling price that you would make you happy. It is the point at which you have won the auction as a seller. The goal in all of our tactics in choosing various auction options is to get a bid at the winning price.

The lowest, acceptable selling price may not be attainable. The lowest price you would be happy with for your autographed Napoleon letter about the Italian campaign is $2,500, but it may be that no one is willing to pay that amount in the venue of an online auction. The winning move in this situation is not to offer it for sale online. Sell it elsewhere, but don't try to auction it off on eBay, Amazon, or Yahoo!.

The steps in setting a minimum starting bid or reserve selling price begin with establishing your winning price, estimating the most that it can be sold for on your auction site of choice, and verifying that your winning price is below that likely maximum. Once the winning price is established and seems to be reachable, then some strategy comes into play when setting the starting price. Here are the recommended steps for setting a starting price:

1. Establish your *lowest, acceptable selling price.* What is the least that would make you happy? Don't forget to add in all the costs of running an online auction before calculating your winning price.

2. Estimate the *probable selling price* on your chosen auction site. The best method is to search the site for similar items that have sold recently (in the last 30 days). In many cases, of course, you can't find an exact match. There is only one autographed Napoleon letter like the one you are offering, but there will be similar *items of type*—other Napoleon memorabilia, other letters of similar historical importance, and so on. Find out what these items sold for (in a successfully completed auction) or what the highest bid was at the end of an unsuccessful auction. Also check your library and real-world auction catalogs to see what actual sale prices have been realized.

3. Compare your lowest, acceptable selling price to the probable selling price. If the lowest, acceptable selling price is greater than the probable selling price, don't list your item.

4. Choose a starting minimum bid somewhere between the lowest, acceptable selling price (your happy price) and about 10% below this price.

The strategy in Step 4 has only a small risk attached to it. You might sell for less than your "happy" price, but you may be willing to occasionally settle for just being "content"—especially if you are picking up skills and experience along the way. The risk of selling for less than your minimum hoped-for selling price is, in my view, small because if this price is below the probable selling price, there will be plenty of bidders out there. In fact, if your winning price is far below the probable selling price (which may be the case for some collectibles you have had for a while or picked up cheap), you'll have so many interested bidders that your computer may burn up right there on the desk! The reasoning behind listing your starting bid slightly below your winning price is to create a little momentum toward getting that first bid. As we discussed in number 6, "Sniping—Going, Going, Gotcha!" window shoppers are more likely to click and examine an auction if someone has already bid. Getting an early first bid is a key element to a successful auction.

Though I've never tried it myself, being the timid type, friends tell me they have had great success with so-called *penny auctions,* where they chose a starting bid of just $0.01 (or some other ridiculously low starting bid) in order to get the ball rolling. Though you might think you risk losing money with this approach, friends tell me that their profits have far outweighed losses because winning bids actually tended to be higher. Try it a few times with a well-designed listing, and see if this method will work with what you sell.

> **NOTE** When checking the highest bid on an auction run by someone else that didn't result in a sale, don't be misled. The last bid registered in a reserve auction where the reserve price was not met will only be one bid increment above the previous high bid, regardless of the amount the most recent bidder entered. The highest bidder may have entered an amount much higher than is shown. Treating that high bid as an estimate of the amount the bidder was willing to pay is the best bet.

19 Naming Your Game

Because this book is about strategy, examining the reasons for choosing any of the various auction formats should be useful. There are good reasons to select *any* of the formats presented in number 17, "Auction Wrinkles," and I suppose there are even a few reasons to consider a reserve auction. Check out Table 19.1.

TABLE 19.1 Auction Formats

Auction Format	Reason to Choose
Standard	Almost always the best choice.
Reserve	To get some quick first bids. If you choose this format, you should always have a very low, minimum starting bid. Reserve auctions without low, minimum starting bids have no use. To test the market and estimate your item's value. You can pay the listing costs and find out how high bidders are willing to go.
Dutch	You have more than one copy of the same item—100 widgets or 8 new copies of the latest Tom Clancy bestseller. This way, you only pay for one auction. Your starting price should be your *lowest, acceptable selling price.* A key tactical decision with Dutch auctions is how many to offer—too few and you haven't used the listing efficiently, too many and your bid won't increase.
Private	You think people might want to keep their User IDs secret when bidding. Use this format for very high ticket items, for some gift items, and for items of an adult nature.
Buy Price	To encourage the impulse that drives most auction purchases. When you know the fair market price and want to sell at that price. When you are in a hurry and want a quick-ending auction.
Auto-Extension	To encourage competition among bidders and create the excitement of a live auction.
Restricted Access	To prevent minors from even seeing your listing. When your listing contains a photo that includes nudity, for example, like a nude painting or a Playboy magazine cover.

20 Aren't I Supposed to Make a Profit? Maybe...

The advice in this book will differ slightly from advice given in a how-to business manual in one way. Here we treat profit as a *possible goal of playing*, but not the *only* possible goal. Power selling is not limited to professional businesses. You may well be one of those mixtures of seller and collector who would like to make as much as possible, of course, but who will probably put much of your proceeds back into your collectibles buying fund. If that's you, this chapter is for you. My objective is to relieve your guilt if you want to sell something at auction and don't care how much you get for it—as long as it is something or, more accurately I guess, as long as it is more than the cost of running the auction.

I occasionally teach an online course about buying and selling on eBay. A while back, one of my students reacted in a way that surprised me at first. In retrospect, I realized that the reaction was a common feeling. A thread through the class postings for the course dealt with ways to get the highest possible bids, how to make sure you don't sell for a loss, whether to set a reserve price to protect yourself, and so on. After a couple weeks discussing various tips and tricks, this student posted a simple question:

"I don't understand this concern about 'protecting' yourself. Don't you want to sell the item? Isn't anything you get OK, since you want to get rid of the item?"

This student was operating out of a perspective that:

1. You have something you don't want.

2. You can sell it.

3. If you get any money for it at all after subtracting the costs of the listing, you have made a "profit" because now you have something you do want.

This is a common approach taken by collectors like myself. I have bought many cool things through auction sites over the years. Some of them, for one reason or another, are no longer valuable to me, so I sell them at auction. Although I certainly want to get as much as possible, it is OK with me if I take in less money than I paid to get the item originally because now I have that money and I use it to bid on some new collectible that I am sure I will never get tired of. (By the way, I still haven't heard from any of you who might be interested in the *Betty and Veronica* cover I mentioned in the introduction. It's still available.) This is the *Garage Sale philosophy*. The same strategies for power selling will apply; it is only the definition of profit that has changed. If this sounds like the reason you are selling your stuff, then it is perfectly appropriate for you to decide your *winning price* based on the "just enough to make it worth it" method.

21 Answering Questions

Auctions last a few days from beginning to end. During that time, you could take a long nap or a slow boat to China, but being near your computer would be a good idea. You may receive e-mail and questions from potential bidders, and no response from you virtually guarantees a lost customer!

Questions don't always come in during an auction, but when they do they tend to fall into these categories:

Condition   Could you tell me a bit more about what shape the item is in?

Policies   Will you ship to China? I'm on a slow boat and hope my item is there when I arrive.

User Identity   Are you the same RedSquirrel231 who sent me the nice collection of Ancient Egyptian sawdust and forgot to wrap it in plastic with an acid-free backing board? If so, you sound cute. What are you wearing?

Item Identification   Your listing describes your Alex Ross' Crisis on Infinite Earths poster as original art. Isn't it actually a lithograph?

Requests for Pictures   Could you send a file with a photo of your car so I can see what you mean by candy apple red?

You should respond to these inquiries quickly, professionally, and with a good attitude. Hopefully, that is the same way you would treat a face-to-face customer in a retail setting.

Potential buyers can get your e-mail address in a couple of ways:

◆ You can include it in your listing (either as text or as an HTML link).

◆ Users can track your e-mail address down on the auction site.

Some sellers choose their e-mail addresses as their User IDs, which is a pretty good idea, if your e-mail address is as pithy and simple as your User ID probably would be.

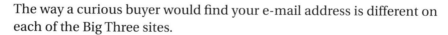

NOTE   To include your e-mail address as an HTML command directly in your listing description, use this text: `<a href="mailto:youraddress @yourprovider">User ID</a>` Substitute your e-mail address for `youraddress@yourprovider` and your User ID for a "Mail Me" phrase where indicated. When a user clicks this link, her e-mail application or her browser's e-mail utility will open with your e-mail address inserted on the "To:" line.

The way a curious buyer would find your e-mail address is different on each of the Big Three sites.

On eBay, clicking your User ID will bring up a screen where they may request to see your e-mail address. Only registered users may access this information and only one User ID can be retrieved at a time.

On Amazon, the request page is accessed in the same way as on eBay. However, anyone can see the information, not just registered users.

On Yahoo!, it is more difficult for potential buyers to contact you. The site recommends that you provide an address yourself when someone asks a question on the Ask The Seller A Question page. You can post a reply that includes your e-mail address. Yahoo! provides free e-mail addresses to all its users, so a buyer might be able to guess your Yahoo! e-mail address from your User ID. Of course, if you don't check your Yahoo! address regularly, you'll never get the mail.

For all three sites, contacting you would be easier for buyers if you just use your e-mail address as your User ID. The potential downside of having your e-mail address so public is that junk e-mail folks can collect it easily. Who knows what offers will begin to flood your e-mailbox!

22 Following the Bidding

Just as the stock day trader rushes to read the *Wall Street Journal* and check a variety of Web sites constantly to get continuous updates on the value of his stocks, you, too, will learn the sorrows and joys of constantly checking up on your list of auctions. Checking the action really is the most exciting part of an online auction. (Though choosing the proper font for an auction listing is a close second.)

You can easily check on your auctions in any of several ways:

◆ The Web sites e-mail you on a regular basis when you are either the bidder or the seller in a current auction. You'll get a summary at the close of any auction for which you are the seller or for which you are the winning bidder.

◆ Software, like the software included with this book, can dial up and automatically check the status of your auctions for you. You can buy all sorts of auction management software to do this chore for you at online auction sites themselves. On eBay, for example, you'll find them in the category of Computers: Software: Internet Related

◆ Some Web sites will track your auctions for you, supply auction software, and provide a host of other auction management services. We discuss these sites throughout the book. For now, you might start by checking out `auctions.goto.com` and the very popular `www.auctionwatch.com`.

◆ An easy and basic way to check your auction is to bookmark your Personal Seller Summary page and check it every time you are online.

My eBay - Welcome idkycdt (0)

Recent Feedback	**Selling**	Bidding	Watching	Account	Favorites	All	Preferences

Items I'm Selling

Item	Start	Current	Reserve	Quant	Bids	Start	End PST	Time Left
Original Art JLA Blackhawk Plastic Man Dillin								See details...
264828145	$39.99	$41.00	-	1	2	Feb-19-00	Feb-26-00 13:52:14	3d 1h 36m
2 drawings - Lucky Charms AND Tony the Tiger								
264856327	$19.99	-	-	1	-	Feb-19-00	Feb-26-00 14:28:50	3d 2h 13m
Beavis and Butthead Original Storyboard page								
265545360	$9.99	$11.50	-	1	4	Feb-20-00	Feb-27-00 12:06:38	3d 23h 50m

Item	Start	Current	Reserve	Quant	Bids	Start	End PST	Time Left
Totals: 3	$69.97	$52.50	N/A	3	6	-	-	-
Totals: 2	$49.98	$52.50	N/A	2	6	-	-	-

Green indicates items that would sell if the auction were to end now.
Red indicates items that would not sell if the auction were to end now.
Click on an underlined column heading to sort in either ascending or descending order.

Here is the My eBay page for my account, User ID= *idkycdt*. My eBay page can be found through links on most pages. You must sign in with your account number and password to access it. You can format this page based on your own preferences. This example shows only the auctions where I am the seller. You can see three items listed, including one of the three Beavis and Butthead storyboard pages that I am using as the Compare and Contrast experiment discussed in number 28, "Location, Location, Location." Each time you go to this page, the status of all your ongoing auctions will update. In this case, we can quickly get the following information:

◆ I am the seller in three auctions. Two have bids, one does not.

◆ Original Art JLA Blackhawk Plastic Man Dillin has received two bids. The current high bid is $41. The starting bid was $39.99. The auction will end in 3 days, 1 hour, and 36 minutes.

◆ The 2 Drawings auction hasn't received any bids and requires a starting bid of $19.99 to play.

◆ The Storyboard page has received four bids. The current high bid is $11.50. The starting bid was $9.99. The auction will end in 3 days, 23 hours, and 50 minutes.

◆ The three items together began at a starting total of $69.97. If the auction ended now, I would sell only two of the items for a total of $52.50.

I can sort this list by any of the columns I want to use. The default is to sort them by item number, which is the order they were entered on eBay.

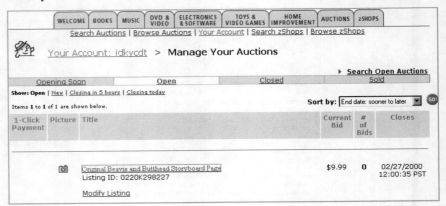

WARNING When you access the My eBay page and other summary pages of auction activity, don't forget to click Refresh from time to time—so you are not looking at the version of the page previously stored in your browser!

Here is a shorter list of the auctions I have underway on Amazon. I can choose to list the following:

◆ Only auctions I have submitted but haven't been posted yet

◆ Only current auctions

◆ Only past auctions

◆ All recent auctions that ended with a sale

◆ Only those current auctions that will end soon

On Amazon, I have only one item up for auction, the storyboard drawing. The current bid is $9.99. This is the starting bid, but no one has bid yet, as the number of bids is 0. The Camera icon next to the title of the auction means that I have included a photo of the item in the listing. As on eBay, you can sort if you have a long list of current auctions based on almost any variable.

ID#	Title	Current Bid	High Bidder	Time Left	To Do
	Welcome, BruceFrey			Submit Item - View Alerts - My Auctions - Options - Sign Out	
	My Auctions			Auctions Home	
	Info - Watchlist - Bidding - **Selling** - Won - Closed/Sold				
18244141	Beavis and Butthead Original Storyboard Page	$10.00	-	3 days	[Manage]

I'm also showing you the Yahoo! listing of my current auctions. Again, the only item listed is the Storyboard page. The starting bid is $10. No one has bid, and the auction ends in about three days. I can choose to see only auctions that have ended. Both Yahoo! and Amazon's summary pages make it easy to modify my listing. On eBay, strangely enough, it is more difficult to modify a listing, and to do so you must enter the item number.

You should keep track of your auctions to see what strategies are working and who is bidding. But you should also monitor them just for fun. It won't be long before you—like millions of eBay, Amazon, and Yahoo! users—are taking a quick daily or hourly peek. It is a blast, especially when you see a bidding war take place and the bids change rapidly! Of course, it is less fun when the bids just sit there, day after day. At least they don't usually go down, like stock prices can. As you become more practiced, the majority of your auctions will be action-packed and you'll look forward to that moment first thing in the morning when you check the ticker to see if the market has discovered your slightly dinged Hardee's Wile E. Coyote glass with no reserve and a low minimum bid!

23 Responding Quickly

Internet technology offers a variety of ways in which you can communicate with potential bidders even faster than you can send an e-mail! If you spend a lot of time online (the average eBay user is on that site for more than an hour per visit) and your customers spend a lot of time online, you can talk to each other pretty easily with *instant messaging* services. Instant messaging allows people to find out when their friends or acquaintances are on the Internet and exchange quick, short messages back and forth. The latest versions of the most popular utilities allow for voice transfer, as well. Typically, users have a number that identifies them. You can give this number out in your listings or in replies to e-mail, and potential buyers can include you in their instant message phone book for speedy contact. ICQ and AOL's Instant Messenger, the most popular tools, are described here, along with some other applications you might explore. All of these are free and can be downloaded to your computer!

ICQ   "I seek you" is simple to use and comes in a variety of formats, depending on your computer platform. Because ICQ is the leader in the field (ICQ is in danger of becoming a generic term for instant messenger), you will probably have good technical support for years to come, and your buyers are probably already familiar with it. Check it out at www.icq.com.

Yahoo! Instant Messaging   You don't have to be on the Yahoo! site to use this instant messenger and, like all things Yahoo!, it's got a potential pool of users in the millions. The services offered rival ICQ fairly well, and it works with a number of other Yahoo! perks. Get it at messenger.yahoo.com.

AOL Instant Messenger   For America Online users (and I guess that's a lot of you!) and for nonusers, too. Find it at www.aol.com/aim.

MSN Messenger Service   Microsoft's instant messaging service includes a feature to let you know when someone is about to send you a reply—which is the ultimate in instant gratification! Get in on the action at messenger.msn.com.

These tools don't have many functional differences between them. There are compatibility problems between the major players, as they hope to shape the market to their product. Try the one of your choice and look me up. (Let's see, I got my ICQ number right here. It's...hmmm...can't find it. I'll get back to you. Promise.)

24 Spotting Troublemakers

Why do you care if someone backs out on a bid? Other than a little disappointment, what's the harm? You can always sell to the next highest bidder. Here's the harm:

Imagine that you have finished a successful auction and finally sold that Brady Bunch lithograph (signed by all six Brady kids, including Marcia who was sick and missed the original convention signing but did later sign a limited number that were sent to her home) for a high bid of $350. You e-mail the winning bidder, who writes back to explain that he is only six years old and didn't have permission to use Daddy's computer in the first place and only has 12 cents in his piggy bank in any case and how could Marcia's signature be authentic anyhow if she was sick the day of the signing? So, Junior backs out of his commitment and you offer to sell to the next-highest bidder, but the next-highest bidder doesn't respond, so you contact the third-highest bidder. The third-highest bidder bid only $75, so you sell to her and get your $75. You are only out a few extra e-mails and a few days of waiting time. Right? Maybe, maybe not. The first two bidders could have been working with the third-highest bidder to drive the bidding up to a ridiculously high amount. The really high bid drove away potential honest bidders who might have been willing to pay more than $75, but weren't willing to pay more than $350. The third-highest bidder might not even have been part of a scheme, but they still win the auction with a lower than market value bid because other bidders made bids they didn't intend to honor. One person can use several different accounts (the Big Three only require that each User ID have a different e-mail address) to manipulate the bidding and won't need to find willing accomplices. This is called *shill bidding,* and it is illegal. Along with being illegal, it is wrong.

Shill bidders are one category of troublemakers. Here are other types of ne'er-do-wells:

- ◆ Winning bidders who never send payment
- ◆ Winning bidders who do not respond to e-mails

◆ Potential bidders who pepper you with abrasive e-mail

◆ Winning bidders who complain that the item they received was not as described when it was exactly as described

WARNING An unsatisfied buyer is not automatically a troublemaker. Some buyers may have legitimate complaints. If you offer a money-back guarantee and someone takes you up on your offer for a legitimate reason, don't be too upset. You told them they could.

If you suspect that illegal activity is occurring, you should report it to the auction site. If for any reason—criminal behavior or just plan trouble-making—you don't want to deal with a bidder, you are allowed to cancel his bid and refuse to sell to him, end the auction early, or do both.

How do you spot trouble? Suspicious bidding behavior is one way. Reading bidder feedback is a great way to spot these folks, as well. It doesn't take long for the eBay, Yahoo!, or Amazon community to spread the word about who's who and what's what. Take the time and effort to learn about your bidders while the auction is still underway. Many sellers have a policy of rejecting bids from anyone with a negative rating. Also, look at other auctions the bidder is bidding in. If they are bidding on the same item in different auctions, they may plan to pay only in the auction with the lowest high bid. Unfortunately, the best teacher is experience, and you may learn the hard way about which bidders are trouble. Refusing to do business with them in the future is certainly okay.

NOTE Yahoo! let's you *blacklist* a bidder and prevent them from ever bidding on your auctions. To do so, use the Add To Blacklist button on the Customize auction page. eBay will suspend the account of a bidder who bids on your auctions after you tell them not to.

Shill Bidding

In the buying section of this book, we looked at how *shill bidding* can hurt bidders. In shill bidding, a fraudulent bid is made by the seller or an associate in order to increase the high winning bid on an auction. A similar method of false bidding can hurt the seller of an item and helps the bidder. Fortunately, from the seller's perspective, this sort of illegal activity is more obvious than the other type of shill bidding. Shill bidding has several warning signs.

It works like this:

1. Two bidders (or one bidder using two accounts) choose an item that is being auctioned at no reserve (or the reserve has already been met) and the current minimum bid is low—substantially below the true value of the item. Typically, the auction still has a long way to go—thus the low minimum bid.

2. Bidder A places the minimum bid on the item and becomes the current high bidder.

3. Bidder B places a bid on the item that is huge—much higher than the likely auctioned value of the item.

4. Bidder B now becomes the high bidder. Of course, the current high bid doesn't increase up to Bidder B's maximum, it only increases one bid increment above Bidder A's bid, but the large bid that Bidder B made is stored as a *proxy* bid in the auction system.

5. Anyone else who comes along and bids is instantly and automatically outbid by Bidder B, through the proxy bidding system.

6. Right before the auction ends, Bidder B retracts her bid. (Bid retractions are allowed, though discouraged, on all of the sites in this book.).

7. Bidder A now becomes the high bidder, with a very low winning bid.

8. If the auction ends with this state of affairs, the seller is obliged to sell the item for a much smaller amount than if the bids of the other active bidders had been recorded during the auction. The bidding history attached to the auction, however, will not show their bids because they were outbid immediately by proxy. At no time were they officially the high bidder.

This bidding behavior is observable, so you can watch for it. The first flag should go up, obviously, when a bidder retracts a bid near the end of the auction. (Bid retractions early in an auction don't work to the advantage of these cheats, and they are unlikely to be the work of shill bidders.) By itself, a bid retraction isn't evidence of shill bidding. It is allowed by sites because there are valid reasons for any of us to need to retract a bid. If you suspect that a bid retraction is the work of a shill bidder, check the feedback on the person who retracted the bid, and also check the feedback on the new, current high bidder, who is probably the person who made the early low bid. Amazon and eBay provide a count of the number of canceled bids made by each user as part of their feedback pages (eBay's count is only for the last six months). If the user in question has retracted bids before (the count is more than 1), then you have even more reason to be suspicious.

If you notice the suspicious bid cancellation before the auction has ended, you can and should stop the auction. The policies of the Big Three sites differ on canceling auctions and are explained more fully in the next chapter. As protection against shill bidders, though, here are the key points:

◆ eBay allows you to end auctions early and cancel all bids, but warns against frequent use of this option. Because you will be notifying eBay and the bidders involved that you suspect shill bidding, however, your auction cancellation will be treated positively, not negatively, by the eBay powers that be.

◆ Amazon's policies suggest you e-mail any current bidders and explain that you have ended the auction early and are not honoring bids. Stricter in tone than eBay, Amazon policy is that you are still obligated to honor high bids for auctions that end early. If you are ending early because you reasonably suspect shill bidding, and notify the site and bidders involved of your concerns, you will be helping the site community and Amazon will support your actions.

◆ Yahoo! allows you to cancel bids and cancel auctions for any reason, but suggests you use the privilege with discretion. However, if you didn't choose the End Auction Early option when you created your Yahoo! listing, you won't be able to end the auction early! As with the other sites, if you end an auction because you suspect dishonest behavior, you should notify the site and the bidders involved.

What if you don't catch the suspicious bid retraction in time and the auction has ended? Do your detective work. Check for a pattern of bid cancellation among the two bidders, and look at their behavior in any current or recent auctions they may have participated in. E-mail the two bidders involved asking them about your concerns. (No response may be evidence that your suspicions are correct.) If your concerns are still not allayed, notify the site and the two bidders that you will not honor the high bid, stating the reasons for that decision. Ask the site to refund the closing fees, if any, and relist the item. If your suspicions are reasonable—remembering that a bid retraction in and of itself is not enough reason to suspect collusion—the sites should be cooperative and thank you for sharing your concerns. Also, regardless of your suspicions, don't forget to leave negative feedback for the bidder who retracted the bid.

A solution to this problem would be for auction sites to store every bidder's maximum bid, even if they were immediately outbid by proxy. If a bid is cancelled, the new high bid could then be calculated and the true selling value of the auction item could be determined without benefiting shill bidders. Even this solution, though, wouldn't re-create the true winning bid that might have been obtained through a free-flowing auction in the first place.

NOTE In the shill bidding process described here, an alternative ploy is for Bidder B to not retract her bid. Instead, Bidder B just does not respond to the seller's e-mails asking for payment. This situation is easier for the seller to deal with, actually, because they are not obligated to offer the item to the second-highest bidder.

WARNING Sometimes, though thankfully it is rare, users just want to seek revenge against sellers. One method is to create many accounts, win many of a seller's auctions, and not respond to any requests for payment. Then, because the user with the many accounts has engaged in multiple transactions with the seller, they can leave multiple mean-spirited feedbacks for the seller. Fortunately, eBay and Yahoo can usually identify the troublemakers once the seller asks for an investigation.

25 Ending an Auction Early

When you list an auction, you have certain privileges and certain obligations. One privilege you have is to end an auction early. Each site has a policy about when you may or should end an auction:

eBay   If an auction has not received a winning bid (a bid at or above any reserve you may have on the item), you may end the auction at any time. You access an Ending the Auction Early page through the Services—Buying and Selling page available at the top of wherever you happen to be in eBay. If there are winning bids, you must cancel them (see the next section) before you end the auction. This action allows eBay to notify these bidders of what you have done. You will be able to explain your reason for the cancellation. You still pay the listing fee, of course.

You may also cancel an auction that has received bids without retracting the bids. Then the item would go to the highest bidder at the time of cancellation.

Amazon   Amazon allows you to terminate an uncompleted auction with a set of rules similar to eBay. If there are no bids, you simply cancel through the Your Account link to View/Modify Open Auctions. Unlike eBay, Amazon does not allow the seller to cancel bids. The site suggests that if you end an auction with current winning bids and you don't plan to honor the highest bid, you e-mail the bidder and explain. "Bidders are within their rights to leave negative feedback and pursue other remedies." Yikes!

Yahoo!   Because it is a free service, Yahoo! has a more liberal cancellation policy. You can end an auction at any time, and you can cancel bids for any reason. The site does suggest, however, that you don't make it a habit. Access the Cancel Auction link through Auction Manager, Yahoo!'s main, personalized auction page.

Why should you end an auction early? There are several good reasons, including:

◆ You change your mind. This is as good a reason as any, I suppose. You can end any auction early guilt-free as long as there are no bids yet.

◆ You lose the item. Sometimes you can literally lose the item; you know that your daughter's prom dress is in the attic somewhere, but suddenly you can't find it. Other times, you only lose access to the item, such as if you were auctioning a friend's property as a favor to him, but he changed his mind.

◆ You break the darn thing! Now, the item is no longer as described. So, if you add an unexpected ding or rip or smudge or chip to your item, you can either just add to the description of the item (an option available on all three sites) or decide to just forget the whole thing.

◆ You learn more about the item, and it isn't really what you thought it was. A typical listing in the eBay category Books: First Editions: Signed often includes additional information added after the auction starts that is some variation of this:

"Thanks to all those who e-mailed to correct my description of the Signed First Edition of the Holy Bible. It is apparently not a true first. Some have also questioned the authenticity of the author's signature."

◆ If you discover some information that changes the quality of the item you are offering, consider simply ending the auction and relisting it with a new description.

You need to remember a couple of points on ending an auction early. If you do it a lot, the powers that be may become annoyed, as will your pool of potential bidders. A bad reason to end an auction early is that you changed your mind about how low you are willing to sell it for. This is unfair to the winning bidder. Legitimate reasons for canceling auctions include restarting an auction that was tainted by illegal bidding activity, discovery that the item is not what you have advertised, and when the auction site goes down and you feel your auction was harmed. Remember to cancel the auction before it ends (I guess, by definition, you can't cancel it after it ends—but you know what I mean). You are bound by legitimate winning bids when an auction ends normally.

26 Canceling Bids

Legally, you can cancel a bid at any time. Ethically, there are four situations where it would be okay to cancel a bid:

◆ You are ending the auction.

◆ You suspect a bidder is not who he says he is, or you can't verify their e-mail address.

◆ A bidder asks you to cancel her bid. This happens occasionally because even though bidders are able to retract a bid, they may write you with an apology and ask that you cancel the bid on their behalf.

◆ You have a policy of not dealing with bidders who fit certain criteria. You might decide that you will accept bids only from bidders with positive feedback, or from buyers in the United States. If these are your rules, you should clearly state them in your auction listings. The first example (requiring that bidders have positive feedback) hurts brand new buyers and limits your market, so I'm not sure it's the wisest business practice, but you can set any rules you feel are best. The auction sites may tire of frequent bid cancellations and could ask you to stop, so whatever your policy, make sure it is defensible.

Amazon, eBay, and Yahoo! allow you to cancel bids, using a multiple-step process.

On eBay,

1. Start at the Services page. Every eBay page has a link at the top.

2. Click Buying And Selling.

3. Click Cancel Bids On My Item.

4. Enter your User ID and your password.

5. Enter the item number. (This is a real bother because you seldom need to actually type this in elsewhere on eBay.)

6. Identify the particular bid you are canceling by entering the User ID of the bidder.

7. Give a reason for the cancellation. (This message is available to the public as part of the bidding history, so be nice.)

8. Finalize your decision by clicking the Cancel Bid button.

Repeat this process for every bid you want to cancel. They don't make this very easy. What does that tell you?

NOTE Notice what the eBay bid cancellation page requires. You need to have a lot of information handy before you go here!

> **Your User ID**: [   ]
> You can also use your email address.
>
> **Your Password**: [   ]
> Forgot your password?
>
> Are you tired of typing in your User ID and Password over and over again?
> Save time by signing in. (You may also sign in securely).
>
> [   ]
> Item number of auction
>
> [   ]
> User ID of the bid you are cancelling
>
> Your explanation of the cancellation:
> [   ]
> (80 characters or less)
>
> Press this button to cancel this bid.
>
> [cancel bid]   [clear form]

On Yahoo!,

1. Starting on any auction page, click the My Auctions link.

2. Click the Selling link.

3. Click the Manage link to go to Auction Manager.

4. Click Cancel Bids and follow the instructions.

You should cancel a bid only after you have carefully thought through the ramifications. It can mess up a clean bidding history and possibly upset potential future customers and the site management. On the other hand, canceling a bid could solve a problem quickly and neatly.

On Amazon,

1. Start at the auction for which you want to cancel bids.

2. Click on Modify Auction.

3. Choose Cancel Bids.

4. Once a bidder's bid has been canceled, the bidder is not allowed to rebid in the same auction.

27 Site Outages and Other Anomalies

A friend of mine used to have an aquarium full of "sea anomalies" and they are fascinating creatures. In this chapter, we'll discuss ways of trading these gentle monsters of the deep for Horatio Alger, Jr. books.

Just kidding. *Anomalies* are unusual and unexpected occurrences and eBay, Yahoo!, and Amazon have had their share. All three sites have been the victims of *hack-attacks*. Pranksters or vandals (depending on your point of view) were able to shut down the sites with a few well-aimed volleys of massive computer-generated requests for information. These sites, and others, couldn't handle the demand on their time and all transactions came to a stand still.

What happens if your auction is disrupted because of some technical difficulties? Yahoo! has no posted policy, and their legal disclaimer specifically claims no obligation to provide service, but the two "pay" sites, Amazon and eBay, have policies designed to help sellers in case of unexpected trouble:

◆ eBay offers an automatic extension of all auctions after an unplanned *hard outage,* which is defined as a period of time when no one can bid. If the outage lasts for more than 2 hours, a 24-hour extension is automatically applied to all auctions scheduled to end during or 1 hour after that time.

◆ Amazon's automatic extension of auctions depends on the period of time that the hard outage lasted. For outages of less than 30 minutes, no extension is offered. For outages between 30 and 120 minutes, the extension is for twice the length of the outage. For outages of more than 2 hours, a full 24 hours is added to the affected auctions.

NOTE You aren't required to accept the extensions due to outages. You may still end the auction if you are happy with how things stand by following the Ending An Auction Early process.

28 Location, Location, Location

When it comes to location, smart sellers like you have two choices to make:

- ◆ Which auction site do I choose?
- ◆ Which category do I choose?

In this chapter, we'll talk about these decisions.

The Great Beavis and Butthead Experiment

Recently, I conducted a small experiment. I found three items that were essentially alike that I wanted to auction. I ran three auctions—one on eBay, one on Yahoo!, and one on Amazon—at the same time to compare and contrast the experience and the results.

Because I sell collectibles, and collectibles tend to be unique (even duplicates are often numbered differently, or vary in condition), the best I could do was find three very similar items. I had a complete *storyboard* of the MTV animated program "Beavis and Butthead." (Let me apologize up front for the number of times I will now have to use the word "Butthead" in this book. Had I chosen another item, I could have avoided feeling like an adolescent while typing this chapter!) A storyboard is a collection of drawings that act as the script for the animators. This storyboard had several pages. I had purchased it as a complete unit (many pages stapled together) some time ago, but I found it difficult to display. I decided that I could sell the storyboard as separate pages, because animation art collectors and other

"Beavis and Butthead" fans might gladly pay $10 or more for a single page. So, I chose three pages that were very close in the plot and had similar graphics.

WARNING   Running three simultaneous auctions with exactly the same item would have been wrong, of course. I would have had to deny the sale to two of the three winning bidders, which is a big violation of auction ethics (and possibly illegal).

With my handy-dandy digital camera, I took photos of the pages and prepared three listings. All listings had the same wording and included a photo. I set a minimum bid of about $10 and no reserve. The Amazon listing is shown here. For each listing I chose the same category (as close as possible). On Amazon, it was Collectibles/Animation/Animation Art.

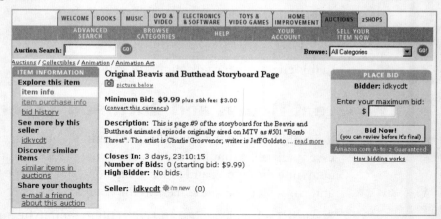

The purpose of the experiment was to gather data on:

Eventual selling price   I assumed this would be only a function of the number of shoppers and the demographics of the Web site users. In other words, the more people who see the listing, the more people who might be interested in bidding. The number of potential bidders, though, isn't as important as whether the shoppers are collectors who are looking to buy or are just there to window shop. I would guess that eBay users tend to be more hard-core collectors than Amazon users (except for books) and Yahoo!. My prediction was that I would get my highest winning bid on eBay.

Communication from the site   All three sites have automated e-mail confirming your listing and updating you on the progress of the auction.

Communication from potential bidders   Amazon and eBay provide your e-mail address, as well, so you can occasionally expect e-mail from interested bidders. Yahoo! encourages you to use the section on your auction listings where you can respond to questions from other Yahoo! users.

Table 28.1 presents the results of my experiment. (This was not a particularly scientific experiment, but it is a good model for the sort of marketplace testing you can do yourself.)

TABLE 28.1   My Experimental Results

Site	Listing Cost	E-mail from Potential Bidders	Number of Bids	Winning Bid
Amazon	10 cents	0	0	No Bids
eBay	25 cents	1	9	$40
Yahoo!	Free	1	1	$10

The e-mail I received from the eBay and Yahoo! users asked the same question. Was the storyboard page, that I was describing as *authentic,* the original art, or a copy that is made during production to aid the animators? My page was a studio copy, not the original art. I realized that I needed to respond to those curious customers and I needed to add the information to my listing—so other potential bidders would have a clearer idea what I was offering. For Yahoo!, I could respond in the Question And Answers section on my listing. On eBay, I added additional information to my listing to try to clarify things. eBay has links on active auction pages that allow you to add or revise information if you have no bids. Notice how additional information is added below the original description. If you have already received bids, you cannot alter your description; but you can add to it. On eBay, go to `pages.ebay.com/services/buyandsell/add-to-item.html`.

Description
This is page #10 of the storyboard for the Beavis and Butthead animated episode originally aired on MTV as #501 "Bomb Threat". The artist is Charlie Grosvenor; writer is Jeff Goldstone. There are a limited number of storyboards produced for each episode. This one is pencil marked as belonging to John A. and dated 11/02/94. The authentic page offered shows Beavis and Butthead at their desks as they become aware that there is a bomb threat. In nice shape; suitable for framing. Add $3 for mailing costs. All my auctions have a two week money back guarantee.
On Feb-24-00 at 11:16:48 PST, seller added the following information:
In response to questions, let me make it clear that this is one of a few copies made for this episode. Only a few copies are produced from the original drawings as an aid in the animation process. This page was used in the production of the episode.

N O T E Be reasonable with bidders when you change or add to the description of your listing. In my experiment, the high bid of $40 came before I added the additional information, so I was prepared to allow that bidder to retract his bid.

Before my experiment, I guessed that I would find the most action on eBay. This turned out to be the case, dramatically so. The eBay user pool is so huge that it doesn't make sense to exclusively use another site.

I recommend that you use eBay when you want the highest bids; however, there are two exceptions to this advice:

1. Because Yahoo! is free and Amazon is almost free, little harm can come from running auctions on those sites at the same time as eBay (as long as they are different items). You might find that your product sells better when aimed at Yahoo! users, for example.

2. Amazon's great strength is their large following by book lovers. I suspect that if my item were a book instead of adolescent animation art, the results would be different. If I were going to auction a valuable collectible book, I'd try Amazon first. Amazon sells retail (I understand there are some people who buy new?). Your auction will be linked automatically to show up when a search term you choose is entered on their retail pages. If it doesn't sell on Amazon, then try eBay. You are only going to be out a dime.

Pick Your Pigeonhole

All of the sites require you to pick a category for your item. The specific categories available overlap a great deal, with eBay leading the way in the variety and number of categories. Strategy is involved when choosing the best category.

Collectibles (1051710)	Toys, Bean Bag Plush (377736)
Advertising (97526)	Action Figures (49721)
Animals (36634)	Bean Bag Plush (70932)
Animation Art (2237)	Diecast (77088)
Animation Characters (21210)	Educational Toys (844)
Art (33624)	Electronic Pets (847)
Autographs (7620)	Fast Food (8154)
Banks (4001)	Fisher Price (4500)
Barber Shop, Shaving (2223)	Games (44240)
Barware (3253)	Hobbies (5489)
Bears (15155)	Kites (132)
Bottles (13366)	Marbles (2921)
Breweriana (24400)	Modern (7225)
Breyer (2414)	My Little Pony (1184)
Casino (5777)	Peanuts Gang (4465)
Chalkware (1387)	Plastic Models (14952)
Circus, Carnival (1787)	Plush (7489)
Clocks, Timepieces (13476)	Pokemon (38827)
Coin - Operated (4871)	Puzzles (2795)
Collector Plates (10147)	Slot Cars (4097)
Comic Books (55395)	Television Toys (2688)
Contemporary (740)	Toy Rings (187)
Cultural (31556)	Toy Soldiers (3501)
Decorative (41766)	Trains (1190)
Dept 56 (4558)	Vintage (11698)
Disneyana (27408)	Vintage Tin (4058)

NOTE The numbers in parentheses after each category name tell you how many different auctions are currently listed in that category. For example, 70,932 different Beanie Baby auctions, 7,620 different autograph auctions, and 55,395 comic book auctions are going on in this example. It boggles the mind!

Keep in mind as you are picking a category that your auction isn't really physically placed in a certain location. Potential buyers can find your item without going anywhere near the similar items available on the same *aisle*, so to speak. The category just determines where your auction will be listed if someone wants to browse through all the listings of a given type. Buyers can also find your auction by searching for any auction titles containing certain words.

Some people search and some people browse. Some do both. It depends on whether a person collects by type, like *contemporary glass paperweights*, or by characteristic, like all things related to the classic old-time radio show "The Great Gildersleeve." The first buyer finds objects by starting on the Browse page and eventually getting to Glass/Paperweights/Contemporary (with 356 current auctions available on eBay!). The second type of buyer starts at Search, which is at the top of most pages, enters **Great Gildersleeve**, and sees auctions from a variety of categories—recordings of radio broadcasts, phonograph records, magazine advertisements, photographs, autographs, and even jar lids. The moral is to choose your category with the browser in mind, but compose your title with the searcher in mind. Where would someone who wants what you have go to find it? Place your auction in the category that most specifically features your kind of stuff. Verify that the other auctions there are selling similar stuff, and you'll know you have the right place.

Top : Pottery & Glass : Glass
Current || New Today || Ending Today || Completed || Going, Going, Gone

Jump to a list of all items in Glass

General (7687)

40s, 50s, 60s (6830)
General (4061)
Anchor Hocking (1335)
Federal (227)
Hazel Atlas (389)
Indiana (249)
Jeannette (232)
L.E. Smith (84)
Libbey (116)
Macbeth-Evans (12)
U.S. Glass (125)

Amethyst (443)

Art Glass (7009)
General (2779)
Bohemian (361)
Czech (405)
English (109)

Depression (11457)
General (4920)
Akro Agate (135)
Anchor Hocking (2085)
Federal (926)
Hazel Atlas (831)
Indiana (645)
Jeannette (1181)
L.E. Smith (70)
Macbeth-Evans (328)
McKee (209)
U.S.Glass (127)

EAPG (1651)
General (1155)
Colored (307)
Flint (109)
Ruby Stained (80)

Elegant (10550)
General (3749)

Lalique (283)
Opalescent (582)

Opaque (1957)
General (273)
Chocolate (22)
Custard (60)
Milk-Blue (92)
Milk-Pink (46)
Milk-White (1374)
Slag (90)

Pairpoint (85)

Paperweights (2174)
General (1378)
Contemporary (356)
Studio (84)
Vintage (356)

Pressed Glass (916)

12 items found for **"great gildersleeve"**. Showing items 1 to 12.

All items | All items including Gallery preview | Gallery items only

Item#	Item	Price	Bids	Ends
274577809	THE GREAT GILDERSLEEVE! 185 GREAT Radio Shows	US $27.00	2	03/09 18:25
275532715	4 Great Gildersleeve TV shows on VHS	US $19.00	7	03/11 06:03
273801968	GREAT GILDERSLEEVE Willer Waterman 3/2544	US $5.50	-	03/11 18:51
276667231	The Great Gildersleeve	US $2.00	-	03/12 15:09
276868104	Tune in The Great Gildersleeve RARE jar &lid	US $5.60	2	03/12 17:31
276884584	Great Gildersleeve Stories For Children 78	US $3.00	-	03/12 18:02
274623262	GREAT GILDERSLEEVE Willer Waterman 3/2544	US $5.50	1	03/12 18:57
277286164	THE GREAT GILDERSLEEVE! 185 GREAT Radio Shows	US $24.95	1	03/13 07:44
277669651	Great Gildersleeve Mystery Baby Contest Ad	US $5.00	-	03/13 17:52
279739435	THE GREAT GILDERSLEEVE! 185 GREAT Radio Shows	US $24.95	-	03/14 12:09
279739679	THE GREAT GILDERSLEEVE! 185 GREAT Radio Shows	US $24.95	-	03/14 12:10
278767662	THE GREAT GILDERSLEEVE! 185 GREAT Radio Shows	US $24.95	-	03/15 07:13

29 Expert Selling Advice

Our panel of real-life, online auction buyers and sellers offer their thoughts on the strategies of selling.

User ID: aaagh!
Category: Comic Book Art

"Look professional! Do everything you can to have better-looking ads than your competitors. My listings are in color, with an illustration of the item (kept to a size no bigger than 50K). I also include links to not only my Web site, but to pages including the history of the products I sell, and tips on how to get the best from them. The pages take no extra time to appear, and the longer you can keep a prospective bidder looking at your auctions, the more chances there is of them putting in a bid. If you are listing many items, list items under different categories and more people will see them. Also consider putting one item a week in the Category Featured section (preferably with a BOLD heading). It'll appear at the top of the category for a whole week, and everyone will see it!"

User ID: xjhawkx
Category: Sports Cards

"The key to selling is to hide nothing. Make sure there is a clear picture of the item, as well as a detailed description. This will ensure a better transaction and virtually eliminates complications. I like to explain how the item will be shipped, the additional cost of shipping, and my return policy on items."

User ID: ssabellico
Category: Star Wars

"A seller needs to be part advertiser, part collector, and part P.T. Barnum. Know what you are selling. Do your research. Compare yourself with other sellers of the same item. The great thing is that eBay is not just a platform for buying and selling, it's also a wonderful research tool. If you have an item that you're not sure about how to auction, do a search on eBay for it. Do a

search for current auctions. See what it's currently being sold for. No listings? Try a completed search to see what people have sold it for in the past. Read which listings got higher bids. Ask yourself 'Why?' Learn from the pros by imitating them."

Expert Summary

Our panel agrees that a good listing needs to *sell* the item, and that the best way to sell the item is to provide all the information that a buyer needs to make up her mind. Additionally, sellers can use online auction sites as a research tool to learn about items and how to sell them.

Closing the Sale

In the real world, you only have to worry about a few things when a customer walks out of your store. Is anything missing? Will her check clear? Will he be a return customer?

In the Web world, you are pretty safe from shoplifters (I *think*), but you still have the same concerns about getting paid and building a base of satisfied customers. We will discuss the strategies for power sellers that are put into play right after the end of a successful auction. A good system of quickly notifying the buyer, encouraging rapid payment, and promoting return business is a must for the long-term seller online.

30 | It's All about Trust

On the Web, communication is always a matter of trust. You trust that people are who they say they are. You trust that they are honest. They trust that you are honest with them. In online auctions, both the seller and the buyer must rely on four basic assumptions:

The winning bidder will honor his bid. The legalities of auction bids are beyond the scope of this book because I'm not a lawyer. But what I have learned from the policies of the Big Three auction sites is that placing a bid on an item that you don't intend to honor is a clear violation of the rules and *ethics.* Agreeing to honor a bid implies an agreement to respond to the seller's notification e-mail and to provide payment quickly.

NOTE Amazon and eBay will refund their cut of the selling price if a winning bidder backs out. Just notify customer service through e-mail and ask for your refund.

NOTE Your obligation to provide feedback about a particularly good customer extends to providing feedback about a particularly bad customer, as well. Let other sellers know when a high bidder refuses to honor the bid, by adding negative feedback to the bidder's profile.

The auction listing includes all the relevant information. Obviously, nothing in the listing should be misleading. However, this assumption also means that there are no important omissions. The item's condition should be described fully enough for the buyer to picture accurately what will be received. All required fees should be described in the listing. Any mandatory policies (like "money orders only") should be listed.

WARNING If you provide a photo of your item, you aren't relieved of your obligation to describe any important damage or defects. You can't be sure that the photo, as displayed on the bidder's computer screen, shows enough detail to inform bidders or displays the right colors.

The bidder's check will clear. This is a metaphor for the assumption that the high bidder will actually pay for the item. The buyer must write a check which is good, not contest a credit card charge they have authorized, and actually mail that money order. Buyers and sellers trust that both parties will obey the laws governing the exchange of money for goods.

The seller will sell. The seller's most important obligation is to go through with the sale. Why wouldn't a seller honor her obligation to sell? After all, to quote my former *Buying and Selling on eBay* student again, "Don't you want to sell the item?" Sometimes sellers list an auction and then have seller's remorse when an item doesn't go for as much as they wanted. Other times, sellers list an item only to collect information from the bidders—to build an e-mailing list or to get a sense of the item's value. You may have noticed by now that one of the primary buying and selling strategies presented in this book is to do the right thing. When you offer your full-sized, cardboard Austin Powers standee for a starting bid of one cent, you are promising to sell it for any bid of a penny or more.

Trust is always important in a successful business. It is even more crucial in the business of Web auctions where both the buyer and the seller are essentially anonymous and invisible. SafeHarbor, eBay's collection of protection resources, is a model for the Web auction industry and will provide you with the avenues to increase trust and provide some good food for thought. Check it out at:

`http://pages.ebay.com/help/community/index.html`

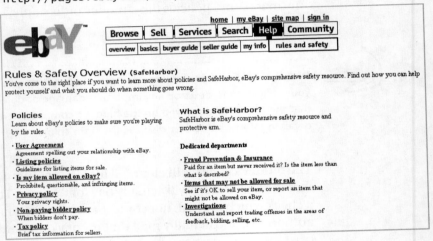

31 Spotting Potential Problems

As any experienced buyer or seller will tell you, the huge majority of sales are trouble free. Unfortunately, the few troublesome auctions can cause enough angst to overshadow the many good experiences.

What are the early warning signs of potential trouble immediately following a sale? Here are a few:

The winning bidder has a brand-new User ID.   Auction users on all three sites can change their handles whenever they want—or simply create a new identity with another e-mail address. If a user has a brand-new ID, it might mean that they decided to improve it, wanted an individual identity apart from a group handle they used in the past (like for a whole family or company), or are new to the site. Or it might mean something bad. It could mean that the user is trying to hide from a past identity that may have had a bad reputation. Perhaps because of the "shady" possibilities, eBay displays an icon showing a pair of sunglasses to indicate that a user has created their current User ID in the last 30 days. All sites let you check the User ID history for any user, and you can get a quick snapshot of a user's history by doing that.

NOTE   Feedback follows users who change their IDs, so shady characters can't really run from their pasts. If you change your nickname (as opposed to creating a completely new identity), your new identity will have the same comments and rating attached as your old identity did.

The winning bidder has no feedback.   This means the buyer is probably brand new. Newbies may not have learned the system and the standards of appropriate behavior. On the other hand, at least they don't have negative feedback. Maybe you'll be the lucky first seller to leave them some!

The winning bidder has negative feedback.   Read the feedback. Is there one negative comment? Are there many negative comments mixed with many positive comments? What is the overall nature of the comments? Many sellers have a policy of refusing to sell to buyers with negative feedback. At least, read the feedback and don't rely just on the number before making this decision.

The winning bidder does not respond to e-mail.   This is particularly frustrating. This feels like you are talking to someone who is ignoring you! The auction site policies require communication between buyers and sellers in the first few days after an auction ends. If the winning bidder doesn't reply to your e-mail, you can treat this as a refusal to honor the bid, in most circumstances, and offer the item to the second-highest bidder. How long should you wait for a first response? After you send your first notification to the winning bidder, wait three days. Send a second attempt and wait three more days. The second attempt takes into account a weekend where the winner may be away from his e-mail, as well as a few more days for courtesy. After a second attempt without a response, offer your item to the second bidder, and leave negative feedback for the first bidder: "Winning bidder did not respond to e-mails."

NOTE   The auction sites themselves will send e-mail to winning bidders letting them know that they have won, but you can't rely on this notification to nudge the winning bidder into sending you e-mail. You must send your own. For whatever reason, this site-generated notification can be very slow. On eBay, likely because of the tremendous volume, notification has been known to take several days.

The winning bidder asks questions about the item after the auction is over.   This is a subtle concern. If I get e-mail back from a winning buyer asking for further information about the item, I start to get worried. Why did he bid if wasn't sure about what he was bidding on? My worry is that the questions may be laying the groundwork for an eventual bid refusal. I love answering questions during the auction, and even after the auction, but sometimes the winning bidder is just looking for an excuse not to pay. Answer the questions honestly with a smile—and keep your fingers crossed.

The winning bidder delays a commitment to send the money.   With a good buyer, the process works like this: You send her an e-mail telling her she won, how much she owes, and asking for a confirmation. She sends you an e-mail saying she will send the money right away. Any response other than that and you start to get a sinking feeling. Maybe she plans to pay, but she needs time until her next paycheck or would like to wait until the end of the month. This is generally okay with me in the rare circumstances when someone requests it. But maybe she is stalling because she doesn't plan to pay up and just isn't saying so.

The winning bidder delays payment.   This is the worst! All has gone well in the post-sale follow-ups, but the money just does not arrive. Is it lost in the mail? Was it sent? Can you trust the buyer's e-mails professing ignorance as to why it hasn't arrived? It is an awful feeling, primarily because you can't be sure of the buyer's guilt or innocence. The truth is that letters seldom get lost in the mail. If you haven't received the check, it is almost always because it wasn't sent to you. Verify that the buyer used the right address and remain polite, but don't feel guilty. It's not your fault that the check hasn't arrived. (See number 38, "Getting Paid by Checks and Money Orders," for more on handling checks.)

NOTE A nice person like you can't help feeling uncomfortable when telling a buyer that the check hasn't arrived when he insists it was sent. Good people sometimes worry that the buyer might think *they* are not telling the truth. Remember two things. First, you *are* telling the truth. Second, you don't have the check to cash. Until it is cashed, the buyer *hasn't* lost any money.

It is worth repeating that you will rarely have to deal with these early signs of trouble, but an ounce of prevention is worth a pound of cure. (Okay, that's three gems of advice you have gotten, so far: 1. Buy low, sell high. 2. Choose eBay as your primary auction site. 3. An ounce of prevention is worth a pound of cure. I think you and I both know you have easily gotten your 20 bucks worth with this book!)

32 Collecting Information

Record keeping can make the difference between a good seller and a great seller. As you build your Web auction business, you can collect lots of information about your bidders—both winning and nonwinning—and about your successful and unsuccessful auctions. You can build a list of past buyers who might be interested in catalogs (either by e-mail or snail mail) or a listing of your current auctions.

NOTE Some sellers regularly e-mail their past customers with catalogs or other promotions. This can be a great business tool, but online auction rules require that recipients *opt-in* to these promotions. You must get their explicit permission before mailing. Don't be responsible for sending junk e-mail and lose your auction privileges!

Here is the information you should collect on your winning bidders:

◆ User ID

◆ E-mail address

◆ Mailing address

◆ What they bought

◆ What they owe

You can track your winning bidder on the Web auction sites by using only his User ID. This is his identification for all practical purposes. Until you know his real first name, you can refer to him using this nickname, you can check his feedback, leave him feedback, see what other items he is bidding on, and see what items he is selling.

Searching for the auction activities of others is simple:

1. Go to the eBay search page, for example. Use the link at the top of almost every page.

2. Search for the User ID of a seller or a bidder by clicking the appropriate button.

3. You will get a complete list of his activities.

I searched for a list of auctions where `4allkids` is the seller, by entering that User ID requested on the Search-By-Sellers page. ("For All Kids" is a charity sponsored by the Rosie O'Donnell television show, which auctions off items given to Rosie by guests on her show.) I can see a complete listing of all their current or past selling activities. To see their bidding activities, I can search *By Bidder*.

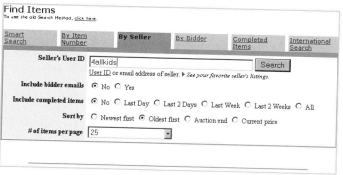

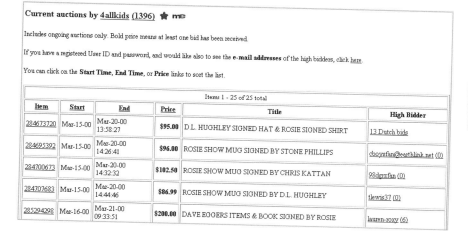

Item	Start	End	Price	Title	High Bidder
284673720	Mar-15-00	Mar-20-00 13:58:27	**$95.00**	D.L. HUGHLEY SIGNED HAT & ROSIE SIGNED SHIRT	13 Dutch bids
284695392	Mar-15-00	Mar-20-00 14:26:41	**$96.00**	ROSIE SHOW MUG SIGNED BY STONE PHILLIPS	cboysfan@earthlink.net (0)
284700673	Mar-15-00	Mar-20-00 14:32:32	**$102.50**	ROSIE SHOW MUG SIGNED BY CHRIS KATTAN	98dgrzfan (0)
284707683	Mar-15-00	Mar-20-00 14:44:46	**$86.99**	ROSIE SHOW MUG SIGNED BY D.L. HUGHLEY	tlewis37 (0)
285294298	Mar-16-00	Mar-21-00 09:33:51	**$200.00**	DAVE EGGERS ITEMS & BOOK SIGNED BY ROSIE	lauren-roxy (6)

You'll need the buyer's e-mail address so you can notify him of his winning bid. Your notification from the Web site that the auction is completed will include the winning bidder's e-mail address. If the auction has ended and you have not received the official notification e-mail from the site, you can still look up the e-mail address on eBay or Amazon by clicking the User ID, as listed in the high bidder slot on your auction listing. You will need to be logged in (on Amazon) or provide your ID and password (on eBay) to get this information. eBay's form is shown here.

User ID History and Email Address Request Form

eBay kindly requests that you submit your User ID and password to view the User ID History or email addresses of other users.

Note: When the shades icon 😎 appears next to a User ID, it signifies that the user has changed his/her User ID within the last 30 days. The shades icon will disappear after the user has maintained the same User ID for a 30-day period.

Your User ID: [   ]
You can also use your email address.

Your Password: [   ]
Forgot your password?

Are you tired of typing in your User ID and Password over and over again?
Save time by signing in. (You may also sign in securely).

Where is the "Remember me" box? Please Sign In first, then go to My eBay Preference tab to set/change your preferences.

[Submit]

When you send your notification e-mail to the winning bidder, you should request an e-mail response with her mailing address so you can prepare the packaging while you await payment. If she doesn't provide it in her response, hang on to all the paper, envelope, or anything else that came with her payment so you can hunt for her mailing address. This is the easiest thing to lose track of while you are waiting for the check to clear.

Because you are selling more than one item at a time, you need to link the buyers' names with the items they won. Buyers may not identify which auction they won when they send payment. Although all the auction sites provide identification numbers to distinguish each unique auction listing, you will find it easier to keep track of the item by a brief description of it. Perhaps you can use the auction title.

NOTE Remind your buyers that they must provide their mailing address and the auction numbers of the items they have won, or some other way of identifying the correct auctions. Without this information, do not cash their checks.

You should keep track of the total selling price, winning bid plus postage, and other agreed upon charges.

> **N O T E**   You can even get the mailing addresses of nonwinning bidders, but you should not pursue this option. Internet users deserve privacy, and they don't need their mailing addresses distributed willy-nilly (or to Willie or Nellie, for that matter). Keep in mind the site prohibitions against sending unsolicited commercial e-mail to online auction users. Noncommercial, helpful, and friendly e-mails sent to bidders on your own auctions is generally okay.

Ledger Domain II

In number 11, "Keeping Track of Your Items," we saw a ledger for buyers to use to keep track of their purchases. I recommend a similar accounting method for sellers that summarizes and tracks all sales. The ledger need not have the information on the buyer, as you have saved that elsewhere (either on a separate ledger, or simply in the e-mails you print out or save on your hard drive), but it should include the User ID. The ledger itself can be electronic or on paper, whichever you prefer, and it might look like Table 32.1.

TABLE 32.1   Seller's Ledger

Item	Buyer/ Total Price	Confirmation Sent	Buyer Replied	Payment Received	Check Cleared	Item Sent
6 Avenger paperbacks	Lisa451 $13.03	2/11/00	X	2/17	X	3/1
"Hate Genius" Doc Savage	DrSavage Jr $10	2/11/00	X	2/16	X	3/1
"Starman Jones" Heinlein book	Jlb@dxs. org $13.50	2/11/00	X	2/16	M.O.	2/17
Mike Grell artwork	SuzEQ2 $41	3/10/00	X			

TABLE 32.1 Seller's Ledger (Continued)

Item	Buyer/ Total Price	Confirmation Sent	Buyer Replied	Payment Received	Check Cleared	Item Sent
Shadow Comic Book	LurksOW $108.49	3/11/00	X	3/14		

With a ledger like this, you can easily tell the status of every sale. I know whether or not I sent a confirmation e-mail, got a reply, and received payment. The *Starman Jones* book, for example, was paid for by money order, so I sent the package immediately. The more auctions you have going at one time, the more a ledger like this is a necessity.

The sites provide summary pages, like the one shown here, for all the auctions you are running. By printing them on a regular basis (every few days, or every day that an auction ends), you can use them as a backup or starting document for your sales ledger.

				Items 1 - 25 of 25 total	
Item	Start	End	Price	Title	High Bidder
265423004	Feb-20-00	Feb-27-00 09:25:52	$88.01	Shock Tales #1 Vintage horror magazine 1959	deearenn (61) ☆ (*)
265423011	Feb-20-00	Feb-27-00 09:25:53	$9.99	Saturn #1 Science Fiction Magazine from 1956	No Bids (*)
276730646	Mar-05-00	Mar-12-00 16:06:42	$119.99	Reed Crandall, Vintage, Original Art, WW II	No Bids (*)
276730631	Mar-05-00	Mar-12-00 16:06:42	$104.01	Quest of the Spider 1933 Doc Savage Hardback	gadmark (373) ★ (*)
276730665	Mar-05-00	Mar-12-00 16:06:43	$124.50	Original Sunday Korean War strip! In color!	searchman-1 (272) ★ (*)
276941494	Mar-05-00	Mar-12-00 18:37:44	$9.99	Vintage Sci-Fi Mag Vargo Statten #1 1954	hblad128 (128) ★ (*)
276941483	Mar-05-00	Mar-12-00 18:37:44	$19.99	Vintage 1800's Magic Leaflet De La Mano	ecrow60 (7)(*)
276941539	Mar-05-00	Mar-12-00 18:37:45	$9.99	Vintage Monster Mag For Monsters Only #1	thechoop (9)(*)
278028544	Mar-07-00	Mar-14-00 09:42:54	$10.53	Six Avenger paperbacks - Doc Savage creator	herrick@feist.com (49) ☆ (*)
278028536	Mar-07-00	Mar-14-00 09:42:54	$127.50	45 Doc Savage paperbacks. Instant Collection!	butner@ilcdover.com (104) ★ (*)
278028558	Mar-07-00	Mar-14-00 09:42:55	$23.50	Doc Savage Omnibus #6 - Four complete novels	cshaw@cybertours.com (8)(*)
278028566	Mar-07-00	Mar-14-00 09:42:56	$7.50	Doc Savage PB- Red Spider - #95 - Scarce	ljj821 (5)(*)
278028561	Mar-07-00	Mar-14-00 09:42:56	$8.00	Doc Savage PB- Hate Genius - #94 - Scarce	captain_future (53) ☆ (*)

Using Software to Collect Information

You can use the online auction software on the CD attached in the back of this book to automate a wide variety of your information gathering tasks. The following programs are included on the CD:

Auction Wizard   Auction Management software

Auction Trakker   Sniping, bidding, and record keeping

Virtual Auction Ad Pro   Auction listing design

In addition to helping you find and update information online from auctions, these tools allow you to store monetary and inventory information for all your sales and purchases. With these programs, you can easily snipe and design HTML listings. The comprehensive accounting and record-keeping tools in these applications will help you automate these tedious tasks. Throughout this book, I highlight a few of these software capabilities, but these highlights are only a sampling of what they can do. So take the time to explore these powerful applications thoroughly. As an example, this illustration shows the main Auction Details page from the Sales Manager menu in Auction Trakker where you can enter and store information on each auction sale.

33 Reminders and Other Ticklers

We have assumed that you always send an e-mail to the winning bidders letting them know that they won the auction. This is a good practice, but let's see the steps for all communication from a seller to a buyer after a successfully completed auction:

1. An auction ends with a winning bidder. If you receive notification from the site, you have the buyer's e-mail address. If you haven't received notification yet, you can get the buyer's e-mail address from the site.

2. Send an e-mail to the winning bidder. Here's an example of what you can say:

   Hi,

   You were the winning bidder in my eBay auction for the Avenger paperbacks. Please confirm this e-mail and send $13.03 (10.53 + 2.50 for mailing) to:

   Bruce Frey
   1234 Main Street
   Heartland, KS 66203

   If you provide me with your mailing address, I can go ahead and prepare the package.

   Thanks for the bid!

   Bruce
   eBay ID: idkycdt

3. When you receive payment, send another e-mail. It might say something like this:

   Hi Lisa,

   I received your check for $13.03 today for the Avenger paperbacks. Thanks for the quick reply! It usually takes my bank about ten days before I know that a check has cleared, and then I will mail your package right out!

Bruce
eBay ID: idkycdt

4. When you mail out the package, send one more e-mail. Here's a good one:

Hi Lisa,

I sent your Avenger paperbacks today. I hope you enjoy them! Thanks for your business, and if you are happy with our transaction, please leave some positive feedback by following this link: (Paste feedback location link). I'll leave you some, as well.

Thanks again!

Bruce
eBay ID: idkycdt

5. You can consider another after you leave feedback, though your buyer may be tiring of all this attention.

Hi Lisa,

I left positive feedback for you. I hope you are enjoying the Avenger paperbacks. If you were happy with how things went, please consider leaving me some positive feedback, as well.

Thanks!

Bruce
eBay ID: idkycdt

Some sellers leave positive feedback when the package is sent; others wait until the buyer receives the item and hasn't complained. We will discuss feedback policies in number 34, "Why Positive Feedback Matters."

If you have your e-mail program and your Web browser open at the same time, including Web links in your e-mail is easy. In your browser:

1. Go to the Web page you want to link to.

2. Highlight the address in the Address window.

3. Copy it into your e-mail.

Using Software to Send E-mail

You can automate a great deal of your e-mail communication following an auction by using the software included with this book. The following example shows how to set up automated e-mail in Auction Wizard:

1. Start in the Ledger window.

2. Choose Options from the File menu.

3. Click the E-mail tab.

4. Provide your name, full e-mail address, and e-mail password where appropriate. Auction Wizard will fill in the other e-mail specifics automatically.

5. Choose the various formatting options which interest you. Most importantly choose the e-mail template you would like to use when notifying winning bidders. (This can be edited, as well.)

6. When you instruct Auction Wizard to e-mail all winning bidders (which is done through the E-mail window), it will follow these stored instructions.

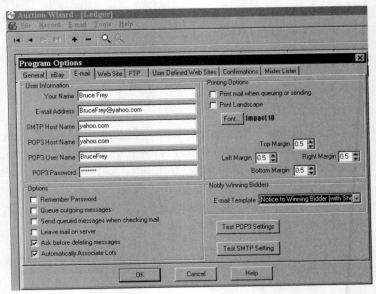

34 Why Positive Feedback Matters

Feedback is a very important part of the online auction world. It is the most crucial trait of sellers and buyers that invites trust and respect. As a seller, you should have a policy defining who gets positive feedback and who doesn't. Tables 34.1 through 34.5 present the various philosophies and the thinking behind each policy. Of course, only you can choose your policy.

TABLE 34.1 Ultra-Conservative Feedback Policy

Behavior:	A seller with this policy never leaves positive feedback.
Reasons:	Positive feedback really only benefits sellers, so buyers don't need positive feedback. The buyer benefits by getting a nice item at a good price; they don't need additional benefits.

TABLE 34.2 Conservative Feedback Policy

Behavior:	A seller with a conservative feedback policy leaves positive feedback for a buyer only when the transaction is unusually favorable for the seller. For example, when the seller made a lot of profit, payment was made very quickly, or payment was made by money order or cashier's check.
Reasons:	Positive feedback is a "thank you" note. In a traditional business, I'd send a nice note to my best customers, but not to all my customers. Positive feedback is a motivator, and I definitely want to encourage this buyer's behavior.

TABLE 34.3   Bilateral Feedback Policy*

Behavior:	A seller with a bilateral feedback policy only (and always) leaves positive feedback if the buyer also leaves positive feedback.
Reasons:	The heart of community is cooperation. "If you scrub my back, I'll scrub yours." "One hand washes another." "It takes two to tango." "Where's the beef?" (The preceding phrase doesn't belong here. I get carried away easily.) I should reward customers who help my feedback rating.

*This is the approach which is most common and is recommended by the sites.

TABLE 34.4   Liberal Feedback Policy

Behavior:	A seller with a liberal feedback policy leaves positive feedback for every buyer at the completion of a successful transaction.
Reasons:	Good behavior should be rewarded. It is a part of good customer service to thank all your customers.

TABLE 34.5   Ultra-Liberal Feedback Policy

Behavior:	A seller with an ultra-liberal feedback policy leaves positive feedback for every buyer as soon as their check clears or payment is made.
Reasons:	A really good seller has above average customer service and trusts that a transaction will go smoothly. If you leave positive feedback, the buyer is less likely to complain about the item after delivery.

Where should you be on this continuum between a very conservative policy and a very liberal policy? My personal position is somewhere between a conservative and a bilateral policy. I believe the argument that feedback is less important for buyers than for sellers, and I also like the idea that part of building an online community is the exchange of support that comes from both parties leaving feedback.

What to Say

Here's an example of eBay positive feedback for a good buyer. (You're looking at him!)

= 1 = [2] [3] [4] [5] (next page)	
User: oh2collect@aol.com (12) ☆ **Date:** Mar-20-00 16:09:17 PST	**Item:** 274398828
Praise: Great buyer, good communication, fast payment! A+++	
User: alsulana (60) ☆ **Date:** Mar-14-00 10:50:45 PST	**Item:** 268659975
Praise: Great transaction, fast payment, friendly e-mails, Thanks Bruce	
User: comiccellar (98) ☆ **Date:** Mar-09-00 20:06:05 PST	**Item:** 262722557
Praise: Fast Payment, Smooth Transaction	
User: koolsool (624) ★ **Date:** Mar-05-00 15:26:26 PST	**Item:** 260435147
Praise: Thanks For The freindly Deal	
User: devans1 (287) ★ **Date:** Feb-28-00 15:19:07 PST	**Item:** 249531117
Praise: Smooth transaction, hope to deal with again.	
User: charlyhoho (231) ★ **Date:** Sep-21-99 19:08:06 PST	**Item:** 155024503
Praise: Bruce sent Zippy fast payment/courteous emails! A pleasure to deal with! AAA+++	
User: mr.mike99 (166) ★ **Date:** Sep-20-99 20:13:07 PST	**Item:** 150755933
Praise: Love this guy, he was high bidder in multiple auctions, A++++++++	

The important issues that sellers typically commented on include:

◆ Quick payment

◆ Friendly e-mails

◆ Smooth transaction (no complaints, questions, or delays in responding)

Using Software to Leave Feedback

The online auction software included with this book makes leaving feedback easier than ever. Not only can you leave feedback automatically, but you can store default messages that you can use over and over again. Here's how to choose a standard feedback message using Auction Wizard, as shown in the graphic which follows:

1. Start in the Ledger window.

2. Choose Options from the File menu.

3. Click the eBay tab.

4. Among the other links that Auction Wizard uses to navigate eBay, you'll see the current Leaving Feedback URL. Don't change or touch this link, just note that it is there. A bit below that is the Default Feed-back window. Enter the standard *Thank You* that you would like to leave for buyers. This is the statement that will be used when you ask Auction Wizard to leave feedback.

5. To actually leave feedback, start at the Auction Lots window.

6. From the eBay menu, select Leave Feedback.

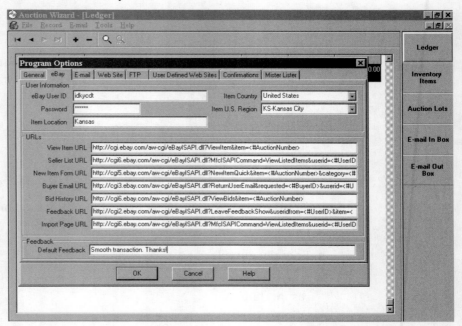

35 **Building Future Business**

Every month or so, I get an e-mail from a seller from whom I bought some comic art in the past. The e-mail is not personalized, but it is friendly enough and usually includes a list of the seller's current auctions with links to each listing. The e-mail begins with information on how I can be removed from his mailing list (by simply replying to the e-mail and putting "remove" in the subject area). I like getting it. I enjoyed looking at some items. The important aspect of the e-mail is that it is not intrusive; it is not a bother.

You can send similar e-mails to your past customers after the sale has been completed. Here's a big caveat before you go e-mail happy: You are required by site policy to get permission before including any user on your mailing lists! They must opt-in before you send them a commercial message that is unrelated to the auction they just took part in. You also should allow them to easily opt-out, as my friend has done.

NOTE Your e-mail software probably allows you to create groups of recipients to receive mass e-mailings. You can compose the e-mail one time and send it to dozens of potential customers. Each e-mail program is slightly different, but typically you name a group and identify individual e-mail addresses that belong in the group. Remember: include only the recipients who have asked to be included.

Here are some other follow-ups you should consider sending:

Thank-you note which includes a link that shows your current auctions On eBay, use this link:

```
http://cgi6.ebay.com/aw-cgi/eBayISAPI.dll?MfcISAPICommand=
ViewListedItems&userid=idkycdt&include=0&since=30&sort=2&rows=25
```

Type it without any spaces and replace idkycdt with your User ID.

On Yahoo, use this link:

```
http://page.auctions.yahoo.com/show/auctions?userID=idkycdt&u=
idkycdt
```

On Amazon, search for auctions by your username to find your personal link. Follow the Search Auctions link to the Advanced Search page, and enter your User ID to find your personal link.

An e-mail which includes a link to your Web site See number 49, "Sending Them to Your Web Site and Other HTML Tricks."

A listing of all your current auctions You can use a list of all your current auctions to cut and paste an e-mail.

A catalog of all the cool stuff you would like to sell!

36 Problem Customers

Here's another one of those discussions with a title describing online auctions as frightening swamps of unpleasantness. They aren't, of course, they are a heck of a lot of fun. But I gotta fill space, so let's examine your rights in the rare event that you do come across trouble.

All of the sites have user agreements. At some point when you signed up, you pushed a little button indicating that you agreed with a long list of rules and regulations. Some of these regulations include your rights as a seller when facing a bad customer.

Seller's Bill of Rights

Although different auction sites have slightly different posted policies, rules, and regulations, certain common-sense seller's rights span all of them, including:

You have the right to leave negative feedback. You should describe only the behavior the buyer engaged in (e.g., *Never sent payment*). You shouldn't attack his character (e.g., *Never sent payment, the jerk!*).

You have the right to use an escrow service. An escrow service is a third party working on behalf of both the buyer and the seller. They hold onto the payment sent by the buyer until the buyer receives the item and is satisfied. Although the major protection is for the buyer (who usually pays for the service), the seller also benefits because he doesn't face the risk of bad checks and other payment mix-ups.

Amazon, eBay, and Yahoo! all offer the same service through i-Escrow, an independent company on the Web. (See number 40, "Escrow Services," for details on how to use an escrow service.) If you are selling a big ticket item, you might require the use of an escrow service to help guarantee a smooth transaction and customer satisfaction. (Make sure you tell potential buyers about this requirement in you auction listing.) You can decide whether you should pay for the service or the buyer should. I recommend that if you require an escrow service, you pay for it. If the buyer suggests it, the buyer should pay.

You have the right to cancel a bid. As we discussed in number 26, "Canceling Bids," you can refuse to honor a winning bid if you do not want to deal with the winning bidder. Be prepared to state the reason in behavioral terms, not personal attacks. Be professional.

You have the right to charge reasonable mailing costs. Some items require more expensive packaging costs, just as some destinations require more postage. Expecting the buyer to pay for these costs is reasonable. Just make sure you state the requirement in your listing, so there is no chance of a misunderstanding.

You have the right to require certain types of payment. As long as it is in your listing, you can require money orders and refuse personal checks.

WARNING It may be your right, but it is not a particularly good business practice to accept only money orders. People who are easily annoyed, like me, may ignore your auction and buy their Beanie supplies elsewhere!

You have the right to refuse the return of an item. Although it makes for great customer service and dandy positive feedback, you don't have to accept the return of an item that you have described accurately. Of course, sellers who are willing to negotiate will prosper, so treat all these rights as privileges you have, not recommendations.

37 Collecting and Paying Taxes

Two tax issues relate to selling though online auctions:

- ◆ Do you pay them?
- ◆ Should you collect them?

The answers are *it depends* and *maybe*.

Paying Taxes

In the United States, you pay tax on any income you receive, and your business income is any profit you have made. *Profit,* for tax purposes, is the amount of money you take in minus the amount of your expenses. Consult a tax specialist for specifics on how much you must take in before you should think of your Internet sales as a business, but the logic is fairly simple. If you made money, you pay taxes. Even if you don't consider your online auction sales a business, you may have *hobby-based income* the Internal Revenue Service would be interested in knowing about. This book isn't a guide for business taxes (and did I mention that I am not a lawyer?), but a few basic bits of advice are worth noting:

As your sales grow, keep records of expenses.   What you paid for an item, the cost of selling, and so on. Typically, collectors have expenses far greater than any profits, so you may not be liable for any taxes at all.

Be careful if you claim your home work area as a home office and, therefore, a deductible expense.   Although the rules governing the deductible expenses of working from your home have been liberalized in the last few years, there are still very strict definitions of, for example, whether you use your computer for work or play and whether your new desk is for business use only.

A ton of good information regarding taxation is available.   You don't even need to be an accountant or a lawyer to understand some of it. A good place to start is the Internal Revenue Service (IRS) Web site, a much friendlier looking place than you might imagine. Visit the taxman at www.irs.gov. The IRS site is also a great source for any tax forms or documents you may need, like the Starting a Business and Keeping Records publication, for example.

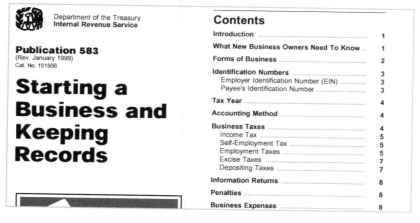

Department of the Treasury
Internal Revenue Service

Publication 583
(Rev. January 1999)
Cat. No. 15150B

Starting a Business and Keeping Records

Contents

NOTE   A particularly good page within the IRS site for folks like you is http://www.irs.gov/bus_info/sm_bus/operating.html. Check it out for answers to many of your small business tax concerns.

Collecting Taxes

The jury is still out on whether products sold on the Internet are subject to state sales tax or not. If they are taxable, which state should get them? Legally, the issue is being debated. The good news is that Congress recently voted to extend a ban on Internet taxes until at least 2006.

The question is whether goods and services sold on the Internet should be treated differently than other products. In the past, products sold through the mail or over the telephone were taxed by the state (if the state had sales tax) where the customer lived. Catalog sales companies collected sales tax from buyers in areas where the company had some physical presence. The problem is that location for an Internet company is a tough thing to define. Is it located where the company is incorporated? Is it located where the products are stored before shipping? Is it located where the server that houses the hard drives on which the Web pages are recorded is stationed? Is it located where the buyer is? Just exactly where is cyberspace? These are tough questions to answer.

So, what do you do in the meantime? If you have a regular store-front business, you must charge sales tax for products you send to addresses within the state where your store resides, just as you do now for face-to-face purchases. Auction listings typically request residents of various states to add a certain percentage of their winning bid to pay local sales tax.

A lot of good Web sources offer the arguments for both sides of this issue and offer suggestions for what a Web-based business should do in terms of tax collection:

www.ecommercecommission.org   The press site for the Congressional committee that explored the issue

www.nettaxfairness.org   Presents one side of the issue (Yes!)

www.handsofftheinternet.org   Presents the other side of the issue (No!)

www.ntanet.org/ecommerce/nta_ecommerce_project.htm   Offers an organized neutral look at the issue

Making the Exchange

Once an auction ends successfully, the real trading begins. You trade away your unopened copy of Microsoft Office software or your orange label Decca Records 45 of *Rock Around the Clock,* and in return you get money. Pretty good trade, eh? This part of the book presents the specifics of getting paid and delivering the item won—which, it goes without saying, should happen in that order. Make sure you have the money in your hot, little hand before you safely mail what was won. Make sense? Good, read on to learn the details.

38 Accepting Checks and Money Orders

As an Internet auction seller, you will usually be paid with a check. There are three types of checks:

Personal Check   You know how they work. The buyer has a bank account, and he fills out a piece of paper which authorizes his bank to give you the designated amount of money. For a check to function, it must include the buyer's bank account number (so the bank knows who he is), the amount of money promised (so the bank knows how much to give), a date (so the bank knows when to release the funds), and the buyer's signature (so it is a binding contract). A check that doesn't include all this information probably will not be honored by the buyer's bank and isn't negotiable.

Money Order   A money order is a certificate that can be exchanged for money. The buyer purchases one from a convenience store, a bank, credit union, or a variety of other locations and often pays a small fee (of up to several dollars). The seller of the money order takes the buyer's cash and agrees to accept the money order in the future and pay its cash value. Money orders have already been paid for and are guaranteed. If you receive a money order as payment, pop the cork and pour the champagne because you just got cash in the mail! You can take a money order to your bank and access those funds immediately. You won't have to wait for it to clear. The money order should have your name on it as the payee. If you receive a money order, treat it as cash and send the item right away.

NOTE Buyers often choose to send money orders because they want the item quickly, so reward their good behavior with quick delivery and positive feedback!

Cashier's Check   A cashier's check (or a bank check) works just like a money order, but it has been issued by a bank. The bank has already transferred the buyer's funds to cover the check. You can treat it as cash. The check should be made out to you. You won't see many of these. When you get one, you'll know it is not a personal check because it will be machine printed and have the bank's information on it, but not the buyer's personal information, and it will be labeled as a "cashier's check" or similar term.

Certified and Registered Mail

With big payments, cash payments, or with payments from particularly cautious buyers, you may receive the funds through certified or registered mail. The sender pays a fee for this service at his post office.

Certified mail is sent with a tiny label, which is detached by the mail carrier as it is placed in your mailbox. This little tag is then saved by the post office as proof of delivery.

Registered mail requires your signature before it can be delivered, and proof of this signature is delivered to the sender. It provides a piece of physical evidence for the sender that you actually received delivery. You'll know if you get registered mail because you must sign for it. Certified mail will still have the vestiges of the label which was removed, so you'll notice that, too.

Non-postal service shippers routinely include tracking information and delivery confirmation. For just a small extra fee—35 cents—The U. S. Postal Service will also track your package when you use Priority Mail. You can verify delivery on the www.usps.com Web site.

WARNING If I were you, I'd give extra care and make sure to e-mail buyers who use registered or certified mail to let them know when the item is on the way. I'd also add a few extra packing peanuts to their packages. These types of buyers mean business and take life pretty seriously. You'd be wise to stay on their good side.

NOTE As a seller, you might occasionally consider certified or registered mail as a form of secure mailing for items which fit into envelopes. These forms of mail fall somewhere between regular mail and commercial entities like United Parcel Service (UPS) and Federal Express in terms of safety, item tracking, and proof of delivery. On the other hand, items that fit in envelopes are often inexpensive and may not be worth the additional fees for these services.

Waiting for the Check to Clear

I have a confession to make. When I used to try to sell my comics through ads in comic book collector magazines, my ads always stated that "checks take two weeks to clear," without really knowing how to tell if a check had ever reached that mystical state of "clearing." Phrases like that made me sound like an experienced comic book seller (or so I thought). I imagined that the bank would give me a call if there was ever trouble, and if some time passed without getting that call, then I assumed everything was okay.

This "wait awhile" system works alright. But it isn't fair to the buyer because it takes forever before you get the feeling that it is okay to send the item. The truth is that the bank won't call if there is trouble—especially if you don't have a business account. You will have to wait for a notice in the mail or, perhaps, until your next bank statement. Here's what is most likely to happen when you deposit a check into your bank account:

1. The amount is credited to your account (usually the next day), though it might not be available for withdrawal until the check clears. Local checks

normally take about three business days to clear. Out-of-state checks can take five to seven business days.

2. The check is sent to the issuing bank.

3. The issuing bank receives the check. If there is enough money in the buyer's account to cover the check, they send this amount to your bank (electronically).

4. If there aren't sufficient funds to cover the check, the check is returned to your bank.

5. Your bank receives the check back and corrects your account (if you received credit at time of deposit) by that amount.

6. Your bank sends the check to you with an explanation that there were insufficient funds in the buyer's account.

So, if the check is good, your bank knows it in just a few business days. If the check is bad, it may be many more days before you know it. With the mailing involved, 10 business days would seem to be enough time to identify bad checks. Thus, the magic "two weeks" that I and others often required.

What should you do if you get a bad check? You haven't mailed the item yet (have you?), so the only financial harm may be a fee your bank charges you. My bank charges me five bucks if I deposit a bad check. E-mail the buyer telling him politely what has happened: I'm sorry, but your bank has returned your check with an "insufficient funds" notice. Almost everyone (except me, of course) has made a mistake and written a check which could not be covered, so don't assume you are dealing with a crook. Offer to send him the check and ask him if he would still like the item. If you redeposit the check, you are taking another five-dollar risk, so decide if it is worth that risk.

NOTE Asking the buyer to reimburse you for any banking fees you suffer when you deposit a bad check is appropriate. Don't hesitate to ask for it to be included in any second attempts to pay for the item.

Online Banking

Many banks now allow you to have Internet access to your account. This is a huge boon to the "wait two weeks with fingers crossed" folks like me because you can log on each day and see what is happening with your account. In the case of deposited checks, you can see when the deposits are credited, track any debits or "corrections" to your account balance due to a bad check, and watch for any debiting or banking fees resulting from bad checks. If your bank doesn't offer this service, it probably will soon. In the meantime, your automatic teller machine or push-button phone may provide the same services.

You may also be able to have your bank send checks on your behalf for the auction items you buy, so consider that option if it is available. The small monthly fee charged for this service can pay for itself almost immediately in stamp money alone. But the peace of mind that comes from having an electronic, bank-certified record of my transactions is priceless.

39 Credit Card Payments

If you are a retailer and are already set up to accept credit cards over the phone, obviously you can continue to do that with your auction listings. But what about the rest of us? All major online auction sites provide a service to sellers that allows them to accept credit card payments. Independent Web services also offer such services.

A credit card transaction has two parts:

1. Authorization and capture, which checks to see if enough credit is available to cover the purchase (and reserves that money)

2. Batching, which actually transfers the funds

When you use your credit card to buy a pair of shoes at the mall, the funds are not transferred from the credit card company to the retailer on the spot. The transfer is only authorized and reserved. Online credit card processing essentially combines Step 1 and Step 2. As Internet sellers, we are interested in services that give us Step 2 capabilities.

Credit Cards on Yahoo!

The Yahoo! site offers just about any service you can imagine. To accept credit cards for your auction sales, you can choose the level of service that matches the volume of your online sales. An economy-sized service for folks who don't need a whole store of their own (and few of us do) but who want to allow credit cards for their Yahoo! auction sales is available for $29.95 each month. The service is called Order Manager, and it provides some customizing options for buyer e-mail and listing displays. Credit card transactions are available online, and for your monthly fee, you can have unlimited credit card transactions. Create your Order Manager at:

```
http://st0.yahoo.com/RT/SIGNUP-AUCTIONS
```

Yahoo! Stores is a resource where you set up an online shop, which becomes part of the Yahoo! community. As the seller in a Yahoo! auction, you can run your auction sales through your Yahoo! shop, and you can include links to your auctions in the shop, as well. As a shopkeeper at Yahoo!, you can process credit card orders online using a link to First Data, an online credit card processing company. There are no charges for the credit card processing, but there is a monthly charge for your Yahoo! store. Here is the fee schedule:

$100/month   You are allowed 50 items for sale at one time, or links to 50 auctions.

$300/month   You can have 1,000 items for sale at one time.

>$300/month   For an additional $100 a month for each additional 1,000 items, you can have as many items for sale as you want.

Welcome, brucefrey	Account Info - Sign Out
Yahoo! Auctions	

Getting Started

- See Sample Store
- User Guide
- How to Sell Online
- Contact Us

Create Your Own Yahoo! Auctions Account

All you have to do is fill out this form, and you can start building your auctions order manager right now.

1. Choose an id for your account. The id must be a single word: it can contain letters, dashes, and numbers, but nothing else. (Example: `acme`)

Note: This becomes the address of your site, and you can't change it, so choose carefully.

`idkycdt`

2. Enter the full name you want for your site. Here you can type whatever you want. (Example: `Acme Electronics`)

`I Didn't Know You Could Do That!`

3. Click on Create, and we're off.

`Create`

If you already have a merchant account with a credit card, you can still use that account and accept online credit card payments through Yahoo!'s Order Manager. Tell your credit card bank you need a new "MID/TID pair." They will need this information:

Product Name: Yahoo!

Store: FDMS (g/w)

Product ID: 819001

Vendor Name: Yahoo!

Vendor ID: 190

Credit Cards on Amazon

On Amazon, you can choose to accept payment from winning bidders through Amazon.com Payments. Payments for items are made to Amazon online with a credit card, and the money is transferred to your account automatically. Signing up for this option places an icon in your listing letting buyers know that they can pay with a credit card. Amazon charges you for each transaction based on this formula:

$0.25 plus 2.5% of the transaction amount

Through the end of the year 2000, a buyer who pays through Amazon is not charged closing fees—the fee for a successful sale. Another benefit for you is that all transactions through Amazon are guaranteed for up to $1,000 automatically. Start the signup process at:

```
http://s1.amazon.com/exec/varzea/subst/buying/
one-click-signup.html
```

Because Amazon is waiving closing fees for auction items paid for with a credit card through Amazon.com Payments until December 31, 2000, you can save substantially on most auction sales if you get the winning bidder to pay Amazon directly. The credit card processing fee that Amazon charges you is less than the standard closing costs for a winning auction.

Amazon.com Password	******

Title	First Name	MI	Last Name
Dr.	Bruce		Frey

Home Phone (913) 555-1212

Daytime Phone (816) 555-1212

To ensure that only you can access your account, we need some important information. As always, we are committed to protecting your privacy.

Social Security # (First 5 Digits Only) 452 - 25 - xxxx
Why is this needed?

Date of Birth Feb 11, 1968 (yyyy)
Why is this needed?

Security Question What is your favorite song?
Why is this needed?

Security Answer She's a Bad Mamma Jamma

Terms of Use ☑ Yes, I have read and agree to the Terms of Use and authorize

Credit Cards on eBay

Billpoint, eBay's credit card service, began in mid-2000 and charges fees based on whether the seller is at the standard or merchant level of sales. A standard seller does less than $1,000 in sales in a month (that's most of us), while merchants do $1,000 or more in each month. Table 39.1 presents the fees schedule.

TABLE 39.1 Fees Schedule

	Transaction $10 Or Less	Transaction Greater Than $10
Standard	$0.39	$0.39 + 3.9%
Merchant	$0.35	$0.35 + 3.5%

The rates here are higher than Amazon's, and they could be higher or lower than Yahoo!'s flat rate depending on your volume of sales. Because it is a newer service, they will probably offer promotions allowing for discounted use, so watch for opportunities such as free service for Visa transactions.

Independent Online Credit Card Services

If you don't want to use the services offered by eBay, Amazon, and Yahoo!, you can try plenty of Web companies who will provide that service for you. Some allow you to accept credit card transactions directly—you take the number and send the transaction. Others act as middlemen—the buyer pays them and you are paid afterward by the company.

If you want to accept credit card payments in the traditional way, where buyers give you their credit card number and authorize you to use it, here are a few Internet credit card services to consider. These providers all charge fees for the service, and some require that you have a Web site that collects the processing information:

◆ AuthorizeNet at www.authorizenet.com

◆ Electronic Merchant Accounts at www.merchantaccounts.net

◆ Merchant Accounts Online at www.merchant-accounts-online.com

◆ Online Credit Corporation at www.onlinecreditcorp.net

◆ Online Merchants Corporation at www.onlinemerchantscorp.com

◆ SecurePay at www.securepay.com

◆ Setup Business Online at www.setupbusinessonline.com

There are also credit card services that do not require you to collect the credit card information. They collect the charge data and process the cards themselves. Two of these services are BidPay at http://bidpay.com, where buyers purchase a money order online using a credit card and then you receive the money order, and the very popular PayPal at secure.paypal.com, which collects the credit card payment for you and sends you the funds.

With BidPay, the buyer pays a fee of between $5 and about $16 for a money order which is sent to the seller. As a seller, this isn't really an option you choose; it is chosen by buyers because it gives them the convenience of using a credit card. It does not provide the normal, speedy delivery advantage of using a credit card because the seller still waits to receive the money order before shipping. Additionally, because buyers are using a credit card to buy a money order and are not technically using that credit card to buy an auction item, they may not enjoy the protection of repayment for a transaction gone bad—"charge back"—they would have if they were paying the seller directly for a product.

PayPal doesn't charge a fee for either the buyer or the seller (unless you are selling as a business). They profit because they earn interest on the money for the brief period of time after they charge the buyer's credit card and before it is withdrawn by the seller. Unlike the credit card services offered by the Big Three sites, PayPal sellers must manually include information about the option in their listings, if they want to advertise the fact that they can accept credit card payments. For many users, this little bit of additional labor is worth the savings they get by not using the online auction credit card services.

40 Escrow Services

Bidders who want to use escrow should, as a courtesy, check with the seller before bidding. (See number 36, "Problem Customers.") Sellers who want to use escrow should include the preference in their listing descriptions. Let's look more closely at escrow services—what they are, how much they cost, and how to use them.

Escrow services offer more security for seller and buyer during an online trade. Escrow works like this:

1. The winning bidder sends payment to the escrow service.

2. The escrow service notifies the seller that payment has been received.

3. The seller sends the item to the winning bidder.

4. The winning bidder notifies the escrow service that the item has been received and meets with her approval.

5. The escrow service sends payment to the seller.

All of the Big Three online auction sites recommend i-Escrow (and provide a direct link) when buyer or seller wants to use this service, so I'll describe the policies and procedures for i-Escrow, but remember that other companies provide a similar service at a similar cost.

i-Escrow

The cost to use i-Escrow may be paid by either the buyer or seller and depends on whether payment (for the auction item) is made by credit card or cash (check or money order), as shown in Table 40.1.

TABLE 40.1 Cost of Using i-Escrow

Transaction Amount	Fee for Credit Card Transaction	Fee for Cash Transaction
0 to $100	$2.50	$2.50
$100.01 to $25,000	4% of transaction amount	2%
$25,001 to 50,000	4% of transaction amount	1%
More than $50,000	Not Allowed	1% (Maximum Fee is $1,000)

WARNING Although the buyer and seller decide who should pay the i-Escrow fee, the seller will be charged the fee if the item is not accepted by the buyer and returned to the seller.

One of the two parties involved in the transaction must be a registered member of i-Escrow, and membership is free. After registering as a member, any transaction the user wants to be sent through escrow must be entered on the i-Escrow site. E-mail will be sent to the other party notifying them of the escrow request and the registered transaction.

NOTE When creating a new transaction at the i-Escrow site, the seller can choose an option to make shipping costs nonrefundable to the buyer.

Email Address: charlie@cia.gov

Product Information
We currently do not accept transactions for Real Estate, Memberships, Tickets, Online Accounts, Weapons, or Perishables.

Description: Silly Otters Comics#1 in Near Mint (signed)
(Example: PowerPC G3, 4.1G, 64M Ram, no monitor)

How did you find out about i-Escrow: eBay

Inspection Period (business days): 2   (we recommend 2)

Details

Your transaction does not currently include line item detail.
Add Line Item Detail

Fees
Calculate your i-Escrow transaction fee.

Purchase Price: $900   (in US Dollars)
(Please do not add the i-Escrow Service Fee. It will be automatically computed and added to the transaction.)

Who pays i-Escrow fee: Seller   Claim Code: 1234

Although using a quality escrow service offers almost full-proof security, at least two potential disadvantages should be considered before requiring it:

1. Escrow costs money.

2. Requiring escrow places an extra step and a bit of extra labor on the part of both parties.

Although escrow provides some protection for the seller (no bad checks or disputed credit card charges to deal with), it primarily benefits the buyer who only has to pay for an item after she has actually seen it and held it and verified it is as advertised. The buyer typically requests escrow, and so the buyer typically should pay for it, but that is negotiable between the trading parties. A fair compromise is for the cost to be split and the buyer's share to be included in the purchase price.

A seller should consider escrow if she is dealing with a buyer who has a history of trouble when making payments and the amount of the profit is worth the escrow fee. A buyer should consider escrow when:

◆ The amount of the purchase is large. The amount is up to you; we all have our own comfort level with Internet transactions.

◆ The condition of the item is the primary reason for its value. Grading the condition of collectibles is a very subjective process, and honest people can disagree. If you only want the item if it is exactly as described, then escrow may be for you.

◆ The seller's identity or location is difficult to verify. If you have suspicions because the seller wants you to mail to a Post Office Box and won't give a street address for verification, or requires a money order (which is harder to trace than a check), escrow may relieve your concerns.

In addition to i-Escrow at `www.iescrow.com`, here are some other online escrow services to consider:

◆ Buyers Assurance at `www.buyassured.com`

◆ Buyers Guardian Escrow Service at `www.buyersguardian.com`

◆ D&M Internet Escrow Service at `www.int-escrow-serv.com`

◆ Escrow.com at `www.escrow.com`

◆ Internet Clearing Corporation at `www.internetclearing.com`

◆ Secure Trades at `www.securetrades.com`

◆ TradeSafe at `www.tradesafe.com`

41 Shipping Safely and Securely

I can't think of anything more important for an online auction seller than quality packaging. Scan through any seller's feedback, and you'll see the emphasis that buyer's place on how safely and securely the item was packed. I categorized a large sampling of seller feedback on eBay and found that specific comments on aspects of the transactions distributed themselves this way:

Speed of Transaction	34%
Quality of Packaging	30%
Good Communication	18%
Accurate Item Description	10%
Condition of Item on Arrival	8%

Speed of transaction is clearly important to buyers and will be one factor we consider in number 42, "Different Ways to Ship." After speed, packing quality is most important. If we assume that the condition of the item can be related to quality packaging, 38% of customer satisfaction can be controlled by careful packing alone. This is the single largest factor in producing happy customers.

Packing and shipping require three components to protect the item and ensure that your 1965 Disneyland Haunted Mansion poster or your Art Nouveau Poppy Majolica Portrait Vase arrives in the same condition in which it left. Those three components are:

- ◆ Protective Covering
- ◆ Protective Packing Material
- ◆ Mailing Container

Many collectibles lie around the house in some sort of container which keeps them in good shape. Comic books are often kept inside an acetate sleeve with an acid-free cardboard backing board. Baseball cards are in plastic holders. Beanie Babies have coverings for their tags and little boxes that the creatures can live it. Collectors who care about quality place their collections in some sort of fairly permanent archival environments. If you sell an item to a collector, it should be shipped in that protective holder. A customer who receives an item out of its plastic coating may think the seller doesn't care about quality.

Once an item is placed into a container for mailing, it often requires an extra ingredient to keep the item extra-safe during mailing. For fragile stuff, packing peanuts, tissue paper, or crumpled-up newspaper provides a cozy and safe bed inside the box. For flat paper goods, a sturdy piece of cardboard taped directly to the protective covering usually does the trick

The rule-of-thumb is that if you are mailing something that's two-dimensional (flat), put it in the appropriate protective covering and sandwich it between or against cardboard; if you are mailing something that is three-dimensional (not flat), put it in a box surrounded by soft stuff. There are the odd collectibles that have their own traditional, mailing methods (like some paper collectibles which can safely be rolled up in a tube), but this rule covers almost everything else.

Because packing materials can add to the weight (and cost) of mailing, the trick is to find the lightest material that still provides the benefit. Another cost is the material itself, whether it is pieces of cardboard or those ubiquitous peanuts. Cardboard can often be cut to the correct size from scraps of boxes you have around the house or saved from the packaging in items you receive through the mail. You can buy packing peanuts, if you need to. They are included in the cost of using a private mailing support service (e.g., Mailboxes, Etc.). But I bet you can find newspaper to crumple-up pretty easily and, as an extra bonus, feel good about the recycling!

NOTE Popped popcorn is a cheap, fun, and perfectly functional packing material that will ensure a smooth ride for the most fragile of vases. For obvious reasons, as my editor points out, plain popcorn works better than buttered.

Everything in this world can be sent in either a box or an envelope. Most flat things, except for the very large, can be sent in an envelope. Most "not-flat" things, except for the very small, should be sent in a box.

Envelopes can be padded or not padded. Padded envelopes are sturdier and have a coating of bubble wrap inside. (Note to the reader: If the last comment isn't followed by two pages and one graphic on the pleasures of popping bubble wrap, then an editorial decision was made that was beyond my control.) The bubble coating protects contents not only from bumps during shipping but from rubbing and gouging during opening. If you are shipping a flat object that is already in a hard protective holder, a padded envelope isn't necessary—although it does look professional.

NOTE After your first make your few sales and have experimented with different sizes of padded envelopes, decide on a size which is just big enough to snugly hold whatever it is you sell and the cardboard you include. Then buy that size padded envelope in bulk at your local office supply superstore. You'll save a good 40 percent from individual purchasing or from purchases at the post office or mailing services outlet, and there will always be a package around when you need one.

Boxes of the correct size can often be found for free. Here's why:

◆ The U. S. Postal Service and private package delivery companies provide as many free boxes as you want if you use their premium delivery services. You can ask for them ahead of time and have them around when you need them. Do your packing at home, and then mail them out at your convenience.

◆ When you buy items online (and almost all sellers do), they often come in boxes. Keep 'em. Clean 'em up. Use 'em again.

◆ Retailers throw boxes away everyday that are exactly the size you need, and not all of them smell like beer. (Okay, most of them do.) Investigate your neighborhood and see what might be possible to gather regularly.

If you can't find your packaging supplies for free, they just aren't quite right, or you become a high-volume seller, consider ordering everything you need for packing from wholesale suppliers. Here are some to consider:

◆ Allied Shipping and Packaging Supplies at www.asapi.com

◆ American Box Company at www.americanboxco.com

◆ American Paper and Packaging at www.americanpaper.com

◆ Box Brokers at www.boxbrokers.com

◆ Box City at www.boxcity.com

◆ Paper Mart at www.papermart.com

◆ Quality Packaging at www.qualitypackaging.com

◆ Ronal at www.ronalproducts.com

Using a Professional Packager

Professional mailing support service companies are open longer and on more days than the U. S. Postal Service. They will pack items for you and provide service with a smile. One reason for the smile, though, is that they charge you money for the convenience. When you buy a stamp, it costs you more than the cover price. When you buy a box, it usually costs more than it would at the post office and certainly more than it would if you bought in bulk. On the other hand, you do get all those Styrofoam bits to fill your box, and they will probably have the right size and shaped container for your needs.

As you start your auction selling career, experiment with your neighborhood mailing service and determine the total cost and convenience of using them. Then compare to something like Priority Mail at the U. S. Postal Service, where you get a free box, and see which is the least expensive. If you appreciate the customer service more at your neighborhood outlet, then decide if it is worth the cost, and whether you will pass that cost along to your customers.

42 Different Ways to Ship

You can choose from a variety of options when you mail an envelope or package. Tables 42.1 and 42.2 present the costs (at this writing) and characteristics of the choices through the United States Postal Service, United Parcel Service (UPS), Federal Express (FedEx) and Airborne Express. Costs are based on typical options (like asking for delivery to the buyer's address, not just to his post office.)

TABLE 42.1   U. S. Postal Service Options

Service	Cost	Delivery Time
1st Class Letter or Package	$0.33 for first ounce $0.22 for each additional ounce	No Guarantee
Priority Mail	$3.20 for first 2 pounds $1.10 for each additional pound	Typically 2–3 Days, but not guaranteed
Express Mail	$11.75 for first 1/2 pound $15.75 for first 2 pounds $18.50 for first 3 pounds About $2 for each additional pound	1–2 Days

TABLE 42.1   U. S. Postal Service Options (Continued)

Service	Cost	Delivery Time
Priority Mail Global (International)	$23 for first 1/2 pound $31 for first 2 pounds $50 for first 3 pounds About $5 for each additional pound	2–3 Days
Book Rate (4th Class Standard Mail)	$1.13 for first pound. About $0.45 for each additional pound	No Guarantee

NOTE *Book Rate* can be used not only for almost any printed matter (excluding advertising), but also for film, recordings, and software. Check with your post office for specifics.

NOTE Remember that for just 35 cents extra, you can get delivery confirmation online with the U. S. Postal Service's Priority Mail.

WARNING Delivery services generally define days as business days. Make sure you know how your delivery service defines their guarantee.

Package Delivery Services

The rates in Table 42.2 are based on typical U. S. delivery distance (my home in Kansas to Beverly Hills, 90210) for a 5-pound package using your own box.

TABLE 42.2 More Delivery Options

Service	Cost	Delivery Time
UPS Next Day Air Early	$56.25	1 Day - 8:00 AM
UPS Next Day Air	$31.25	1 Day - 10:30 AM
UPS Next Day Air Saver	$27.00	1 Day - Afternoon
UPS 2nd Day Air	$13.80	2 Days - Afternoon
FedEx First Overnight	$60.32	1 Day - 8:00 AM
FedEx Priority Overnight	$34.32	1 Day - 10:30 AM
FedEx Standard Overnight	$29.38	1 Day - Afternoon
FedEx 2-Day	$15.08	2 Days - Afternoon
FedEx Express Saver	$13.99	3 Days - Afternoon
Airborne Express Overnight Air Express	Variable	1 Day - Morning
Airborne Express Next Afternoon	Variable	1 Day - Afternoon
Airborne Express Second Day	Variable	2 Days - Afternoon

Note: Airborne hesitates to provide rate quotes because they deal primarily with businesses who have accounts with them. The cost depends on volume.

NOTE For more than just occasional use of UPS and FedEx, establishing an account with them makes sense. You can be billed more conveniently, track your packages easily, and prepare for shipping more quickly. Get started at www.fedex.com/us/registration/account.html and www.ups.com/servlet/services.

Recommendations

The delivery of auction sale items is seldom a time-sensitive emergency! The primary benefit of delivery services like UPS and FedEx is the rush delivery they guarantee. So you would seldom need to use them to deliver your auction sales. These companies have a greater tracking ability though; you can tell exactly where a shipment is at any time—so that would be an advantage. But with certified mail, you can verify delivery with the regular U. S. Postal Service. I recommend that you:

- ◆ Mail all nonbooks weighing more than 12 ounces using U.S. Postal Service Priority Mail

- ◆ Mail nonbooks weighing less than 12 ounces using 1st class U. S. mail

- ◆ Mail most books using U. S. Postal Service Book Rate (4th Class)

If you'd like more information on the rates for your specific needs and destinations, check out the Web sites for the carriers we have discussed:

United States Postal Service	www.usps.gov/postofc
United Parcel Service	www.ups.com
Federal Express	www.fedex.com
Airborne Express	www.airborne.com

NOTE When the postal carrier picks up mail at your residence, she can also pick up Priority Mail packages. You must use special Priority Mail stamps, which are available at your local post office, and the package should weigh less than two pounds.

43 Insuring Matters

With even the best packaging, the item you send may leave in great shape but arrive in bad shape or even not arrive at all. Insurance may make you and your buyer sleep easier at night. The chance of damage or loss is small, though, so paying extra money to protect an item of small value has never appealed to me. (But, hey, that's me, Mr. Vegas!) For larger value items, the small additional fee may well be worth it.

There is also the customer service aspect to consider. If you typically sell items for less than $50, an additional three quarters and a dime is all it takes to provide insurance and to advertise that fact to potential customers. You can include it in the additional shipping cost you add on to the sale price, or simply offer it as an option the buyer can pay for. Unless you are a volume mailer, it does require a trip to the post office for mailing; but if you have a package, not just an envelope, you will be making that visit anyhow.

NOTE The premium rush delivery outfits like UPS and FedEx include some insurance coverage automatically and the extra tracking security they provide is a form of insurance, as well— assurance that the package won't get lost.

The United States Postal Service offers insurance on all deliveries. You can buy up to $5,000 of insurance for most deliveries and up to $25,000 if you use registered mail. You will only get the actual, depreciated value for an item in the case of loss, so there is no benefit to over-insuring an item. Use Table 43.1 to estimate the additional cost for getting insurance.

TABLE 43.1   Cost of U. S. Postal Service Insurance

Your Estimate of Item Value	Insurance Cost
$1.00–$50.00	$0.85
$50.01–100.0	$1.80
Each Additional $100	$0.95

44 Electronic Postage

We (all of us) have finally reached the point where you never have to leave your home. No need to see those annoying "other people" ever again. Congratulations! You can buy and sell through Web auctions. You can get the post office or other delivery service to come by and pick up your packages. You can get all your supplies delivered to your home. And now, you don't even have to leave to buy stamps. You can now electronically download postage from the post office (or, more accurately, through a certified middle man), print it out, and stick it to your package or envelope!

So, what's the catch? E-stamps cost more than the old-fashioned variety. The companies that provide electronic postage add a surcharge of about 10 percent for the convenience. So, a 33-cent stamp is actually a 36.3-cent stamp. Typically, there is a minimum and a maximum monthly amount for this surcharge, as well. So buying in bulk can once again save you money. On the other hand, you get to feel ultra-spiffy-modern for that small fee. There is also the possible additional cost of a printer (which you probably already have) and the sticky labels to print your postage on. Some of the kits include a small label printer which becomes part of your up-front expense.

Here are some of the major e-postage players to consider if you like the idea and convenience of printing out postage as you need it!

◆ E-Stamp at www.estamp.com

◆ NeoPost at www.simplypostage.com

◆ Pitney Bowes at www.pitneybowes.com

◆ Stamps.com at www.stamps.com

N O T E If you like antiques, the U. S. Postal Service will send those old-fashioned, but awfully pretty, paper stamps directly to your home. You can order online at their Web site at www.stampsonline.com.

N O T E eBay offers some freebies in terms of e-postage if you sign up through them with e-Stamp.

Designing a Killer Listing

In the following discussion, we will look at the nuts and bolts of the Internet auction listing. What information is automatically included? What can you choose to include? How can you make your listing more effective?

Designing a powerful listing is an art, not a science. Many of the decisions you make are matters of taste and strategy. Although I certainly have strong opinions on why you *should* include a quick-loading photo and *should not* include animated kitty cats, I would be hard pressed to prove that my suggestions are the only way to go. After all, I do stumble across some apparently successful sellers whose listings:

◆ Are consistently slow to load

◆ Have links that are not active

◆ Have super-huge pictures that tell me nothing more than the color of the drapes visible behind the item up for bid

◆ Are full of twinkling lights and rotating logos

So, you can ignore all the advice to come and still sell your stuff. A good item at a good price is the most important part of any listing. But I truly believe that if you want to maximize the number of interested bidders and maximize their bids, you need a professional, persuasive, crisp-looking, error-free listing. If that makes sense to you, read on....

45 Information Basics

Every listing on any of the Big Three auction Web sites provides the same basic information. What it says is up to you, but the layout of this basic information is, for the most part, out of your control.

Listing formats vary somewhat across auction sites. Here we will focus on just one portion of the listing: the Basic Information section. This is where bidders can find all the basic facts and data that they need to know about an item—well, it's where they can find all the information that can fit within a browser window. Users can scroll up and down the window to see pictures and prettied-up HTML bells and whistles. As you design your listing, you need to ask yourself what information needs to be visible in the same browser window with the all-important I Want To Bid! button. Here are the Basic

Information sections of three separate listings from the Great Beavis and Butthead Experiment discussed in number 28, "Location, Location, Location." Three very similar items (essentially the same item) were put up for auction on eBay, Yahoo!, and Amazon.

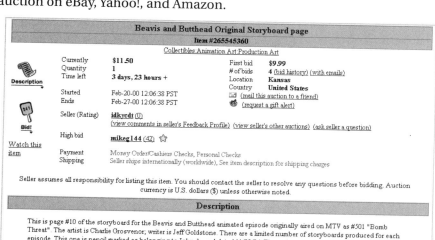

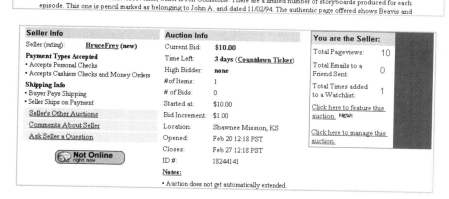

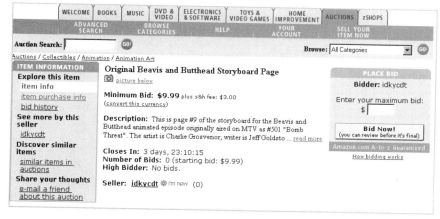

NOTE Only the Basic Information sections of the listings are shown here. Of course, Yahoo!'s listings include auction titles and item descriptions too, but they are included, along with pictures, above (or before) the Basic Information section. A buyer must scroll back up to that information.

NOTE Yahoo!'s listings look different if you are not the seller—a bidding area replaces the You Are The Seller box.

Take a look at the information presented as part of the basic listing. Table 45.1 allows you to compare and contrast the three listing formats. Remember that Yahoo! and Amazon were inspired by (or *copied from*, depending on your point of view) eBay, so one would expect to find very similar components.

TABLE 45.1 Basic Information Section of Listing

Included in Basic Information Section of Listing	eBay	Yahoo!	Amazon
Title	X		X
Auction Number	X	X	
Category	X		X
Current Bid	X	X	X
Quantity	X	X	X
Time Remaining Until Auction Ends	X	X	X
Auction Ending Time	X	X	
Time Auction Began	X	X	
Seller	X	X	X

TABLE 45.1 Basic Information Section of Listing (Continued)

Included in Basic Information Section of Listing	eBay	Yahoo!	Amazon
Seller's Rating	X	X	X
Indication of Whether Seller Is New	X	X	X
Link to Seller Feedback	X	X	X
Seller's Payment and Shipping Policy	X	X	
Link to Seller's Other Auctions	X	X	X
Link to Ask Seller a Question	X	X	X
Link to Add Item to a Watch List	X		
Item Description	X		X
Small Photo of Item		X	X

Make note of which of these functions makes it easier to bid. Remember, this book's philosophy is that most auction bids are spontaneous actions, so layouts that encourage impulsive bidding are exactly what we want. Some components of this Basic Information section that encourage impulsive bidding are:

Current Bid Probably the most crucial stimulus for an impulsive bid, all sites place this information up front.

Time Remaining Until Auction Ends If time is running out, I better bid now!

Seller's Ratings Can I trust this guy?

Link to Seller Feedback Does this seller ship fast? To quote the little brat from the movie *Willy Wonka and the Chocolate Factory,* "I want my Oompa-Loompa NOW!"

Seller's Payment and Shipping Policy If you take a credit card, I can bid right now; otherwise, I better check my bankbook.

Item Description This is where you can persuade the bidder to bid—and to bid now.

Small Photo of Item This nice feature of Amazon and Yahoo! listings places a small picture of your larger picture (also attached to your listing) beneath your title and above the bid. Very seductive!

Yahoo!'s Customized Auction Booth

On Yahoo!, you can format your auctions so that they present the information you want in the location you want. With one visit to your Auction Booth, Yahoo!'s version of your own little area at an antique mall or flea market, you can create a template which will be applied to every auction listing you set up. You can insert a personalized logo in the corner of every page, choose which links are available in the main information area, and insert a link to your personal Web site. (How to place a link to your Web page in your item description, regardless of the site you use, is discussed in number 49, "Sending Them to Your Web Site and Other HTML Tricks.")

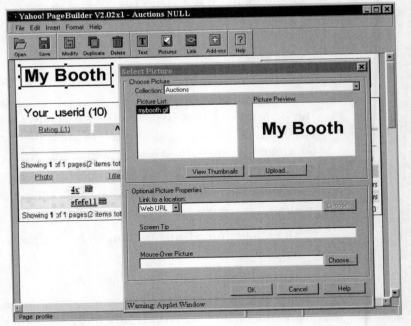

NOTE To insert a link to your Auction Booth on the Yahoo! Auction page, go to the page where you want to insert your link, choose Options and then choose Customize My Auction Booth.

46 Naming Your Auction

There isn't much space available to name your auction. eBay allows 45 characters, including spaces. Yahoo! and Amazon allow 80 characters, including spaces. So you need to choose your words carefully. The winning strategy for choosing a title addresses two objectives:

◆ To make sure your auction is found in a search

◆ To persuade a browser to take a look

Of the two objectives, the first, making sure you're found, should be your top priority. If space remains, you can add certain hot-button words to encourage people to click the listing and take a look.

Helping Bidders Find You

Earlier, we discussed two common ways that bidders stumble across your listing. Remember, there are millions of listings everyday on eBay, and hundreds of thousands on the other sites. With that much competition, getting noticed is hard. If your auction is noticed, it is probably because a buyer was looking for a specific kind of item and typed some search words that matched at least one of the words in your title and you were listed among others in the search results, or they were skimming the hundreds of listings in a specific category. The savvy buyer does both, but the search method is most common. This is why the number one strategy for choosing a title is to use all the key search terms that you think your buyers will stick into the search engines on these sites.

N O T E The advice about using commonly searched keywords in titles applies as well to using the words in the item descriptions. All three sites give users the option to search only titles or titles and descriptions. Yahoo! also has an option to search descriptions only. If you can't get a crucial word into your title, certainly put it in your description.

N O T E Consider using a question mark in your title. "Roseville pottery?" attracts more attention than "Roseville pottery" without the question mark.

Only you can determine the specific keywords you'll utilize for the items you sell. To help you find the right words, ask yourself what words you use to find relevant auctions? Here are some other tips to keep in mind when you pick keywords and develop titles:

Alternative Names or Spellings Will that big bidder out there type *Beanie Babies, Beanies, Beanie Baby,* or some other permutation? Try a title with at least Beanie, so your item has a chance to be included in all these searches—or try 'em all if you have the space.

Title-Category Redundancies If searchers are browsing in the Music:Records:78 RPMs category and they come across your collection of Caruso records, they won't need to see the word *record* or 78 in your title. Other searchers, though, who enter the word *Caruso* as a search term and find your listing may not click it unless the listing includes the word *record*, because they only want recordings. Try a search of your own on a phrase like *Edward G. Robinson* and look at the listings. How many listings don't even state what the item is? Is it a video? A photo? An autograph? A listing can be pretty ambiguous if a crucial noun is missing. Most collectors search for auctions by using keywords, so you should always include an identifying noun to let us all know what the heck it is that you are selling.

Our Celebrity-Driven Culture Famous names are great keywords. If you are selling your copy of *Big Land* comic book, an adaptation of a 1950s film, you will double your potential audience by including the name *Alan Ladd* in your title. He appears on the cover, and now you have attracted both Ladd fans and comic fans. Why not include the word *Western*, as well, for the person who is browsing the comic books category, but only likes stories which involve lots of dust, cattle, and the chaffing that comes from long days on the trail? The same advice goes for fictional characters, too. I buy all things Doc Savage—books, art, toys— so I search for any auction with his name in the listing.

Our Movies and TV Show-Driven Culture   Many collectibles can be grouped by some movie or television show that spawned them. Although there may be Susan Dey fans, and you should use her name in the title of your Susan Dey paper dolls auction, you should also include the term *Partridge Family,* the show for which she is best known (with all due respect to her *L.A. Law* days). Even if the dolls you are selling aren't specifically tied to that TV show, fans of the show may want to bid.

Abbreviating Keywords   Although it is tempting and useful to abbreviate words to save space in auction titles, never abbreviate a key search term because the searcher probably hasn't done the same and your item won't show up in their hunt. It is okay to abbreviate descriptors like NM for Near Mint or NR for No Reserve, because no one uses Near Mint as a search term. (Although I just did, and got 3,761 hits. Lots of high quality stuff out there!) Book collectors, on the other hand, will probably type the entire phrase **First Edition** or **First** as search terms, and will not use FE or 1ED.

Some abbreviations in your field may not show up routinely in listings and listing titles. Browse through the listings in your category of interest to see what they are—CD, LD, LP, and VHS, for example.

WARNING   As the Internet grew and search engines were relied on more and more to find Web pages, a clever (I guess), if somewhat underhanded, ploy to attract bidders became popular. Some sellers place common Web search terms on their pages, even if the term has nothing to do with the content of their sites. A similar strategy involves placing an unrelated, popular auction search term, like *Pokémon,* in a title just to attract some attention to a listing. This is a violation of site policies. Plus, I defy anyone to tell me how this results in bids!

Hot Button Words

If you have the room after using good search terms in your auction title, you can add some appropriate phrases to attract attention. I don't mean phrases like *Look!,* or its Internet-cool counterpart, *L@@k!*—although there are plenty of titles using devices like that. I mean words that convince the potential bidder that you have something worth taking a look at. Here is a quick list of power words that encourage a look:

◆ NR or No Reserve

◆ Near Mint or NM

◆ Original

◆ Authentic

◆ Vintage

◆ Retro

◆ High Grade

◆ COA or Certificate of Authenticity

◆ First Edition

◆ Original Box

◆ Pristine

◆ 3 Days Only

◆ Like New

◆ Unopened

◆ Unread

◆ One of a Kind

◆ Susan Dey or Partridge Family

That last one might work only on me, but you get the idea. It should go without saying, of course, that when you use a descriptor, it should be accurate. At the very least, clicking on an auction only to discover that your Bugs Bunny 7-11 Slurpee cup isn't truly *like new* is annoying.

47 A Few Words Are Worth a Thousand Bids

It's time to develop a specific set of guidelines for writing an item description. Take a look at the description in this eBay listing for a *Shadow* comic book.

Here are the characteristics of the listing that I think make it effective, persuasive, and buyer-friendly:

◆ It is one window big, even on browsers that have pretty small viewing areas. Because the description is brief and includes a photo, a shopper can read the entire description and see the item on one screen without scrolling up and down in their browser window. All the descriptive information (including the picture of the item)and all the qualitative information a potential bidder needs to have can be processed in one look. This makes for a very easy, hands-free viewing process. A buyer can look back and forth from photo to description with the ease of a real-world shopping experience. Additionally, a potential bidder doesn't have to wade through window after window of irrelevant junk—those animated logos we discussed earlier, elaborate background wallpaper, big fonts, formatted links to Web sites, and lots of white space—before they even know what is being auctioned.

◆ It identifies the item exactly. In this case, it gives the title and issue number of the comic book. (Normally, with comic books, only the title and issue number are necessary. However, earlier comic books, like *The Shadow*, renumbered starting with 1 every year. This description gives the volume number and the year to help identify it.) If you are selling a non-collectible or there is no accepted numbering system for your collectibles, use whatever method differentiates it from similar items: year of production, publisher or manufacturer, material it is made from, and so on.

◆ It describes the condition using the vernacular for its category. In comic book terms, *fine-very fine* tells comic collectors that the book looks pretty good and is still somewhat glossy. On the common scale used in the field, it would hold a book value of about 60 percent of the near-mint price. Describe the condition of a new item or a used non-collectible item in terms that compare its qualities to the qualities of purchases made through traditional retail outlets—like new, still wrapped, in original packaging, etc.

◆ It gives condition details. This allows others to judge whether you were accurate in the grading terms you used and also helps to define what you meant. Additionally, this is a good opportunity to teach potential buyers what the common condition words mean to you. "Small crease at bottom right corner and fading" gives a good visual picture of what to expect. It lessens the chance of disappointment when the high bidder opens her package. "Complete with no rips or tears; cover is firmly attached" gives the upside. By the way, these details are not redundant information if you have a picture. You cannot be sure what the picture will look like on the computer screens across the world, and it certainly won't reveal "fading."

◆ It includes one or two "selling words." A little persuasive speech helps a sale, while too much is… well, too much. So a couple of well-placed positive adjectives and reasons to buy are always a dandy idea. Too many selling points, though, is overkill. The persuasive terms in this listing are "beautiful higher grade" and "nice yellow and red cover with a murderous skeleton," What could be more persuasive than a murderous skeleton?

◆ It appeals to buyers in more than one category. Doc Savage collectors who are not interested in comic books might still be interested in this one because it features the start of a series of Doc Savage appearances. (Sadly, this version of the Man of Bronze has him wearing a goofy-looking hat with a hypnotic jewel in the center. That's not *my* Doc Savage, I'll have you know!)

◆ It aims information at the knowledgeable collector. Telling people that this is the first of a series of Doc appearances lets buyers know that the seller is a master of the arcane, just like they are. Nerds, unite!

◆ It has not one, but two photos, one showing the back of the item. These images were combined using simple photo-editing software and uploaded as a single image.

◆ Potential bidders are assured that the seller is an experienced professional. "All my auctions" are guaranteed. Experience equals trustworthiness in the minds of hesitant bidders.

◆ A money-back guarantee is described. The long history of advertising illustrates that guarantees work. Of course, you gotta back it up, but few buyers ever request money back, especially when plenty of condition details are provided in the description.

◆ The mailing fee is reasonable and is linked to well-packaged delivery. The seller needs three bucks, but promises it will be well spent.

◆ Most importantly, it gives a reason to buy. "One of the nicest copies you'll find." Assuming this is true, it is a very appealing pitch.

To summarize, I recommend item descriptions that are complete, but brief, and honest, but persuasive. Whether you are selling comics or fresh off-the-boat lobsters, a good description:

◆ Loads quickly and provides all the necessary information in a compact, easy-to-view area.

- Gives information that identifies exactly what the item is, what condition it is in, and what it is used for (if necessary).
- Sells the item through honest but persuasive language.
- Explains all additional fees, and the fees are defensible.
- Has a picture attached.

Read on to learn how to include a quick-loading, sharp-looking picture to work in unison with a slick description to create a synergy which is hard for impulsive bidders to resist. (By the by, how many other books do you own that include both the phrases "synergy" and "Beavis and Butthead"?)

NOTE Virtually a must-have for tracking interest in your listing is a *counter*. Counters are easily included in your listing HTML code. They provide a visible, running total of the number of hits your auction listing has received. You can often get other information, as well—like the time of day your listing was looked at. Free counters for auctioneers can be found at www.honesty.com, www.manageauctions.com, and www.thecounter.com.

48 A Picture Is Worth a Thousand Bids

The auction gurus agree almost unanimously on one point: You should include a picture of your item. This is so crucial that I am going to repeat it:

You should include a picture of your item.

If you are selling a collectible, a photo proves you have it and indicates the condition it is in. If you are selling something other than a collectible, a photo goes a long way toward duplicating a real-world buying experience. It helps buyers picture the item in their homes.

NOTE Listings with pictures can be featured in eBay's gallery (for a fee) and in a variety of locations on Yahoo! and Amazon (some are free, some are not).

Taking the Picture

NOTE Not every product sold on auction sites is photographable. Software, vacation packages, and so on, can't be meaningfully depicted by a photo. For these auctions, though, you should still include illustrations that explain what the shopper will get if he buys.

Although it is true that Yahoo! is free, Amazon is almost free, and eBay is reasonable, there is an additional cost that is practically a requirement for successful online selling. Digitizing a photograph of your item will cost money. Equipment is the major cost here. (Although if you pay an Internet Service Provider (ISP) or some other Internet service for storage space on the Web that you use only for storing your images for auctions, you should count that as a photo expense, too.) There are three ways to digitize a photo:

◆ Scanning the item

◆ Using a digital camera

◆ Digitizing an existing photo

Tables 48.1 through 48.3 will help you compare them.

A flatbed scanner is perfect for taking a digital picture of flat or almost flat stuff that you'd like to sell. This includes almost all paper and printed material, and also objects that, while three-dimensional, are small enough to be captured (like jewelry, thin books, fabric, pins, and advertising material). The rule-of-thumb is if you can photocopy it, you can scan it. For good scans, avoid highly reflective surfaces and close the cover.

TABLE 48.1   Scanning the Item

Cost:	About $100 or more.
Advantages:	Captures a high level of detail. Stores images on your hard drive, for instant uploading. Inexpensive. You don't usually need to crop (trim) the image. Often comes with image editing software.
Disadvantages:	Cannot scan many, large three-dimensional objects. You must bring your items to it. Scanners are not as portable as cameras. Placing an item between the glass and cover may damage the item. (Try scanning with the cover open if this is a problem.)

Although more expensive than a scanner, digital cameras are dropping in price pretty quickly. Cameras can photograph three-dimensional objects, obviously, and they can also photograph flat material that won't fit into a scanner. Flat objects tend to reflect light back to the camera with straight-on shots, so a scanner may still be a better option, though. You can probably use your camcorder as a digital camera. You'll need an inexpensive attachment that takes the video camera's imaging system (the viewfinder) and uses it to produce digital images, so you may not need to buy a separate piece of equipment just for online auction fun.

TABLE 48.2   Using a Digital Camera

Cost:	About $200 to $900 (but falling fast).
Advantages:	Can photograph anything. You can take the camera to the item. You can choose any angle. Often come with nice photo-editing software.
Disadvantages:	More costly than scanners. Images must be transferred to your computer.

NOTE Most items for sale online do not require ultra-high resolution, so a lower-end camera is probably just fine for most sellers.

Here are some quick tips for taking good photos:

- ◆ Natural light is typically best. A flash is usually necessary only for illuminating deep detail

- ◆ Use a neutral, non-distracting background. Try a clean bed sheet. When possible, use software to trim off the background altogether.

- ◆ Use additional photos to highlight specific details of the item you think are important to buyers.

If you have an old fashioned printed-on-paper photograph (remember those from way back in the 1980s?), you can scan it just like any other piece of paper and digitize it for online use. This works pretty well and doesn't lose very much detail. Another option is working with your film developer. Many companies will now digitize copies of your photos. They usually charge a small fee for this. Your local developer probably offers package prices for developing your film, printing your photos, and placing digital copies of your images on a disk or CD. Keep in mind that film and developing costs accumulate over time, while scanners and digital cameras have no film costs.

TABLE 48.3   Scanning an Existing Photo

Cost:	$100 (for a scanner). $5 to $30 (each time for film and processing costs).
Advantages:	You can use existing photos. No need for a digital camera.
Disadvantages:	Repeated costs of film and processing. You must wait for film to be developed before using it in a listing. No immediate feedback regarding picture quality.

Cleaning the Picture

Once you have a digital image, you can play with it. You can trim it down to remove any wasted background, you can lighten or darken it, and you can enlarge or shrink it. If you are using a scanner or digital camera, you should be able to use the software that came with it to make changes to your images. Digital cameras typically include fairly sophisticated image-manipulation software.

There are two reasons to adjust your digital image before linking it to your auction:

◆ To make it look better

◆ To decrease the *true* size of the image

The true size of a digital image is the number of pixels (the little dots of color which make up the picture) that are required to store your image. The more pixels, the more bytes (storage memory) required, and the more bytes required, the longer it takes for your photo to load when someone is looking at your listing. Big photos take forever to load, and potential bidders routinely back out of any listing that takes too long to appear. A crucial component of a quality listing is a fast-loading picture.

The easiest way to guarantee a fast-loading picture is to make your pictures small. Fortunately, the computer screen and the human eye don't require a lot of pixels to do their work. They don't require nearly as many pixels as digital cameras and scanners arbitrarily assign to an image. A typical digital camera image is 640×480 dots, or even larger, while most images don't need to be even half that size.

The two most popular graphic formats for saving images as files are Graphics Interchange Format or .gif (pronounced "giff") and Joint Photographic Experts Group format or .jpg (pronounced "jay-peg"). GIFs tend to be larger than JPGs in terms of memory storage required, and they are limited to fewer colors. JPGs do a better job of capturing scanned pictures or digital photos because of their ability to store millions more colors, though GIFs may have the advantage if the image is very small. Auction sites recommend that images be saved in .jpg format, which stores the sharpest image.

Take a look at the following picture, taken with a digital camera. It was edited in ArcSoft's PhotoStudio.

The extra space around the salt and pepper shakers isn't needed to show the item. This wasted space is taking up valuable pixels and bytes, and it doesn't provide any information for your bidders. We can improve this photo in two steps:

◆ We can crop it, making it smaller by trimming away the fat

◆ We can decrease the number of pixels it uses to store the image

Now see how the photo looks in a listing. A brief, but complete, description and a nice picture are visible without scrolling up and down. A good rule of thumb for quick-loading pictures is that the graphic files should be less than 20,000 bytes (20K). Some items will require a larger image to show important details, but this standard rule should work well for most auctions. Decide what works best for the type of items you are selling. You can also decrease file size by decreasing the number of colors that are shown. Your scanner or photo-editing software probably will give you this option.

Description
Vintage 1950's salt-and-pepper shakers of Pillsbury's Pop-n-Fresh. A small amount of blue paint off at top back, otherwise in good shape. Add $4 for safe mailing. All my auctions have a two-week money back guarantee.

WARNING When you work with photo-editing software, make sure that when you are shrinking a picture you are truly shrinking it—changing the height and width in pixels. You can select an image and appear to shrink it by decreasing the dotted-line outline around the picture. This may change only how the picture is displayed on your screen, not the number of dots or memory space required to store the image. Check the Properties of the photo to verify its size in pixels.

NOTE Many auctions would benefit by having more than one picture to show the back of an item or a close-up of an important detail. Your photo-editing software should allow you to make two tiny pictures and put them together as one image.

NOTE Plenty of free demo versions of quality photo-editing software are available from providers such as www.download.com. Paint Shop Pro, for example, is a popular shareware program for photo editing.

NOTE If you are planning to be a heavy-duty presence as an auction seller, you might consider buying equally heavy-duty photo- and graphics-editing software (professional quality software like Adobe PhotoShop)—especially if you include photos as part of heavily formatted listings that need some special effects.

Linking the Picture

You need to store your pictures on the Web. When they are shown in an item description or in an auction listing, an HTML command tells the browser to go to the Web address given, retrieve the image, and display it on the listing page. If the image isn't physically stored on an Internet-linked computer, it won't be available. So, to successfully sell online, you've *got* to have access to some Internet storage space. Here are some storage options:

◆ Perhaps you already have a Web page or Web site and are well-experienced at uploading and downloading and editing your pages. If that is the case, then you will have no problem uploading and placing your photos in your own little corner of the World Wide Web and knowing the URL that locates them.

◆ If you have an Internet Service Provider (and let's consider that a necessity) which you use for surfing or for e-mail, you very likely have some free space set aside for you to use. Many ISPs give all their customers 5MB or 10MB of storage space to use. That's enough space to run dozens of illustrated auctions at one time. Check with your provider to see what you can get for free. It is unlikely that you will need more than whatever free space is allowed, until you become a real, high-volume auction ace.

◆ Some Web locations independent of the auction sites will host your images for free. If you don't have a space of your own, consider using www.geocities.com (a Yahoo! site), www.theglobe.com, or angelfire.lycos.com.

◆ You don't need storage space on the Web if you are auctioning on Amazon or Yahoo! They will store the image for you for free! This is a tremendous service, and you should consider taking advantage of it even if you do have your own Web space because you can then dedicate your space to other uses. Yahoo! limits you to 1.5MB per auction and Amazon limits you to 100K per image, but that is more than you'll need.

◆ If you have no Web space of your own and don't want to buy some, there are services on the Web that will provide auction-specific storage space for you for a small fee. Here are a few to consider:

GoTo.com Auctions at auctions.goto.com

PixHost at www.pixhost.com

Pongo at www.pongo.com

Twaze at www.twaze.com

Using an Online Storage Bin

Entering Internet addresses is tedious, especially if your fingers tend to get all tangled. Unfortunately for the typing impaired, these addresses must be entered exactly. When you want to include a graphic or picture in your listing and you are writing the HTML code, you might find it useful to have an online storage area. This is a handy way to quickly check the exact URL for any image you have uploaded to the Internet.

Using your Web page design software, create a table with many cells. Any-time you upload an auction photo or graphic, edit your storage page and insert the image in an empty spot. Because you also keep this storage page on the Web, whenever you are asked to give the URL for an image, you can go to your storage bin on the Web and retrieve the address. On any Web page, you can click on an image and get the image properties, including the URL. Copy and paste that URL directly into the Image Location window on your auction site's Add New Listing page or wherever you would like. In the following storage bin example, you can see that by clicking on the

Poppin' Fresh salt and pepper shakers, you can see and copy the correct Web address.

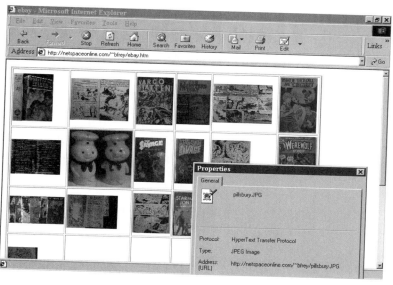

Improving Your Skills

This book focuses on the strategies, tips, and tricks for online auction buying and selling. Unfortunately, we can only skim the surface on the rich topics of photos and graphics, HTML, and Web page development. Many resources full of expert advice on these topics are available. Here are some Sybex books that you should find very helpful:

◆ *Photoshop, Painter, and Illustrator Side-by-Side* by Wendy Crumpler

◆ *Mastering Photoshop 5.5 for the Web* by Matt Straznitskas

◆ *Mastering HTML 4 – 2nd Edition* by Deborah S. Ray and Eric J. Ray

◆ *The Complete Website Upgrade & Maintenance Guide* by Lisa Schmeiser

◆ *Web Pages That Suck: Learn Good Design by Looking at Bad Design* by Vincent Flanders and Michael Willis

49 Sending Them to Your Web Site and Other HTML Tricks

When your browser displays a Web page, regardless of what page it is, it is constantly on the lookout for HTML (HyperText Mark-up Language) formatting commands. These commands, as you probably know, tell the browser how to display the information that is being downloaded from the Internet. The written description you provide for your auction listing is read by everyone's browser when they click on your listing. If it includes any HTML commands, their browser dutifully follows those instructions regarding how to display your listing. This gives you a lot of control over what your listing actually looks like when your potential bidders view it. Just about any formatting you can do in HTML, you can do in the description section of your listing.

I'm about to give you all sorts of HTML commands you can use because that's the kind of thing we do here. As you read about all these super-cool tricks, remember that just because you *can* use them doesn't mean you *should* use them. As my Uncle Joe used to say, "Just because you can make a dozen dancing hamsters drop-kick across the screen doesn't mean you should make a dozen dancing hamsters drop-kick across the screen!" Although many of these format changes can make a listing look good and catch people's attention, they shouldn't be so distracting that you need to scroll forever to find the item described or—and this can be the kiss of death for impatient shoppers—that they take up so many bytes that your listing takes forever to load.

HTML Basics

If you are unfamiliar with the HTML language or if you are over the age of ten, here are some basic rules:

◆ All HTML commands are placed inside angle brackets (< >). They alert your browser to follow the instructions contained within them.

They are the visual equivalent of the "May I have your attention please?" introduction before important announcements at airports.

◆ Most text not enclosed by the angle brackets will be visible on the page. Most text enclosed by the angle brackets is treated as an instruction and will not appear on the page.

◆ Some HTML commands have special words to indicate when the formatting instruction is supposed to begin and when it is supposed to end. They are "on " and "off" pairs of symbols that turn formatting on and then turn it off again. For example, if text is to be centered in the page, the command begins before the text as `<center>` and ends after the text as `</center>`. The slash (/) essentially is a command to end the previous formatting instruction and return things to normal.

◆ Embedding commands within each other is a little like using parentheses and brackets when you solve mathematical formulas. The rule is that you should finish the innermost command first, by using a / , and then end the command which included the first one. For example, to underline and center the single word *Amazing* and then return the format to normal, this order of commands will work: `<u><center>` Amazing `</center>` `</u>`.

◆ Although HTML is used to issue instructions on how to format text, it also was designed to allow for and identify active Web links on a page. Links start with `<a href=url>` (which means *anchor* and *hypertext reference*) and end with `</a>`.

◆ Images are displayed using the command `<img src=filename>` (which means the *image source* is this filename). The source is the name of the file only if it is included in the same folder or directory as the Web page. Otherwise, and always on eBay and Yahoo!, the source is a Web address (i.e., URL, the `http://` address).

The Way You Do the Things You Do

Here are a variety of HTML formatting options, organized by the outcome you want, followed by the HTML code to do it:

Include a link to your home page or Web site.   This command will turn a phrase of your choosing into a link to your site:

```
<a href Put the URL of your site here>a phrase of your
choosing</a>
```

Center the text.

`<center> This phrase would be centered. </center>`

Make the text bold.

`<b> **This text is bold!** </b>`

Put the text in italics.

`<i> *This phrase is in italics.* </i>`

Underline words.

`<u> Underlined </u>`

WARNING   Beware of using the underline command, because underlined text looks like a link to a Web page.

Start a new paragraph.

`<p>`

Drop a full line to move something farther down a page.   It works like a carriage return.

`<br>`

Pick a font color.   Special numbers tell HTML readers what color to make text. Table 49.1 lists the HTML numbers you can use to specify colors. This example uses orange.

`<font color= #FFA500> They'll be orange with envy!   </font>`

TABLE 49.1   Colors and Their HTML Numbers

Red	**#FF3030**
White	**#FFFFFF**
Blue	**#0000CD**
Black	**#000000**
Green	**#00B800**

TABLE 49.1 Colors and Their HTML Numbers (Continued)

Orange	#FFA500
Purple	#8B008B
Yellow	#FFFF33

WARNING HTML allows you to use the name of a color instead of its number (e.g., *orange* instead of FFA500), but the English word will not work on all browsers.

Pick a font size. If you don't like the default font size that browsers will use for your listing, you can change its size.

<big> Increases font size by one level.

</big> Brings things back to how they were.

<font size=+2> Will increase the font size by two levels.

<font size=-1> Will decrease the font size by one level.

<font size=1> Will set your fonts to size "1".

Make lists of numbered items.

<ol> starts the listing format.

<li> each element is surrounded by these </li>

</ol> ends the listing format.

Make lists with bullets.

<ul> starts the listing format

<li> each element is surrounded by these </li>

</ul> ends the listing format.

Place an image in the listing description. You can theoretically place an image anywhere in your description, but it is hard to know exactly how it will look to bidders in relation to the text around it, so it is best to place the image on a line all by itself. So start off with a good healthy <p> or <br>.

<img src= Put the URL of your image here>

Control the size of the image. This won't change the number of pixels (and, therefore, the true size of your image) or its loading time, but it will control how it appears.

```
<img src= Put the URL of your image here WIDTH= "200" HEIGHT=
"100" > or some other values. The numbers are the number of
pixels long or high your picture will be.
```

NOTE Be careful when choosing the height and width of an image. It's appearance will change drastically if your values do not retain roughly the same ratio as the original.

Remove the box that may appear around your image.

```
<img border=0 src= Put the URL of your image here>
```

NOTE Typing the correct Web address every time you want to include an image, or link, is tough. It is much simpler to have your browser open and tuned to the site or image of interest. You can copy and paste the location from the top of your browser to your listing with no chance of typos.

NOTE If you see something cool in a listing and wish that you knew the HTML code to do it yourself, it is right there in front of you. Your browser should let you see the HTML code attached to any page. Perform a quick copy and paste to make it yours to use. In Netscape, choose View ➢ Page Source. In Explorer, choose View ➢ Source.

NOTE Learning HTML is easier when you can quickly see how the results look. Many word processors include a viewing option that displays the page as if it were being read by a Web browser. If you don't have that option, write your code as a text document (or in a simple word processor like WordPad, which comes with Microsoft Windows) and open that document in your browser.

Here is an eBay listing that includes HTML formatting code. In fact, the entire description section is in HTML code.

The seller used a table to place two small photos alongside the item description. Tables are great for placing elements exactly where you want them. You can make them invisible by choosing a color which is the same as the background. You could create a listing of your own that looks like this one by using this code and simply replacing the image sources, the link, and the text with your own photos and information. Here is the complete HTML code that created this slick looking listing.

The first few lines provide information to browsers about the title of the Web page and set the background color to White. Although these lines are good form, they are not required.

```
<html>
<title>listing</title>
<body bgcolor="#FFFFFF">
```

Next, the centered heading in maroon is presented. HTML uses &quot to indicate the use of quotation marks.

```
<h1 align="center"><font color="#800000">Scarce CD &quot;The
Buskers&quot;</font></h1>
```

The table begins with a border size of 0 so that no border appears.

```
<table border="0">
<tr>
```

An image is placed in the first cell of the first row. The image is centered and sized. The Web address for the image is provided.

```
<td align="center">
<img src="http://www.enterprise.net/cdstorehouse/ebay/cd1_1.jpg"
    width="170" height="150"></td>
```

In the next cell on the same row, some text is presented. The color and style are chosen. One portion of text is left justified. The <strong> command is an alternative to <b>, which makes the text bold.

```
<td><p align="left"><font color = "#800000"> <strong>
Unopened 1996 CD for the Minneapolis two man band &quot;The Bus-
kers&quot;. This is their debut CD and it was produced locally
in limited quantities. Hard to find; great music!
</strong></font></p>
```

Another portion of text is centered.

```
<p align="center"><font color="#800000"><strong>
Add $2.50 for shipping costs. <br>
All my auctions have a two-week money-back guarantee.<br>
</strong></font>
```

A line of text is formatted as a clickable link to the seller's home page.

```
<a href = "http://www.enterprise.net/cdstorehouse/
home.htm"><font color="#0000FF"><strong>Click here for other
hard-to-find
and limited edition CDs.</strong></font></a></p>
```

A second image is placed in the third cell on the first row of the table.

```
</td>
<td><img src="http://www.enterprise.net/cdstorehouse/ebay/
cd_B.jpg"
```

```
width="177" height="159"></td>
</tr>
</table>
</body>
</html>
```

Using Software to Design Listings

The software included with this book makes designing nice-looking HTML-savvy auction listings a breeze. By answering a few questions and choosing from a variety of formatting options, you can produce a properly HTML-formatted auction listing that looks crisp and professional.

Virtual Auction Ad Pro

The procedure for producing a nicely formatted listing in Virtual Auction Ad Pro is simple. Fill in a few blanks, click a few options, and the HTML code you need is written, copied, and ready to be pasted into the Description window on any auction site. Here are the few steps it took to create the Virtual Auction Ad Pro listing which is shown:

1. Start in the Item window. Choose a headline for your listing and a subheading if you choose. Write the descriptive information, including mailing costs and all the usual details. For each of these options, you can choose the size and color of the font.

2. If this is your first composition, go to the Preferences window and provide your name, e-mail address, User ID, and a Web home page if you want to send folks there. You only need to enter this information once, and it will be used for all your future listings. It can be changed easily if you wish.

3. While still in the Preferences window, choose the template you would like to use. A variety of templates are provided that place the elements of your listing in different locations.

4. In the Options window, you can add locations of images and photographs, as well as choose a background color or image. You can also include a link to your current auctions.

5. Click on the Generate Ad or View Ad button at the bottom of the window. This will create the HTML code and copy it to your Clipboard.

It can now be pasted into any auction listing. The View Ad button will open your browser and show you what your ad will look like.

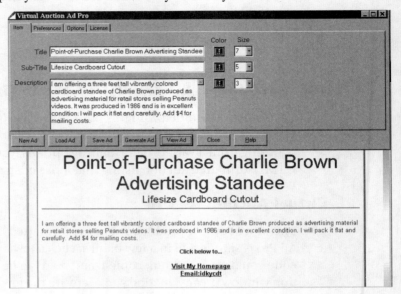

Auction Wizard

Among the many tools available in this comprehensive auction management program is an HTML editing-and-formatting function. The following example shows the middle of the auction listing layout composition process. To design a listing in Auction Wizard, follow these steps:

1. Begin in the Auction Wizard window. Click the Inventory Items button. Add an item to the inventory (Auction Wizard works with *auction lots,* which are made up of inventory items. You must create inventory items and lots before deciding on your listing layout.)

2. Click on the Auction Lots button. In this window, you can do some general editing, as well as provide the auction listing information (title, starting bid, etc.)

3. Choose HTML Template Editor. Now you can use an existing template of HTML formatting information or make your own.

4. Preview how your listing will look by pushing the Preview button.

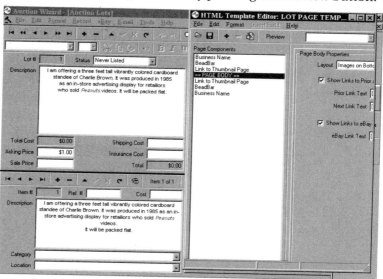

50 Timing the Closing

One attraction of the Internet is that it is there when you need it. You can do all your surfing late at night, and it works just as well as if you set aside your browsing for proper business hours. With online auctions, however, the time of day that you engage in seller activities *does* matter. This is because of one simple fact on eBay and Amazon regarding posting listings. The time of day that your listing is uploaded or posted to the auction Web site becomes the time of day that your auction will end. This is not true on Yahoo!, where you can choose any closing time you want and where you can choose the Auto-Extension option, which keeps the auction going until the bids trickle to a stop. For eBay and Amazon, some tactical planning is necessary.

The closing time is important because so many bidders wait until close to the end of an auction to make a bid. (See number 6, "Sniping—Going, Going, Gotcha!") If that means they have to be up at 3:00 in the morning to do their sniping, then…well, they probably won't stay up, and you can see the problem. If you're one of those people who waits in line at Macy's at 6:00 A.M. to get the jump on the After-Thanksgiving Day Sale, then it may surprise you to hear that the rest of us like to shop when it is a little more convenient, and there aren't many bidders who are browsing around early in the morning. (You and I, of course, can use Auction Trakker to do our last-second bidding for us and still get our beauty sleep!)

When are most snipers on line and ready to snipe? What time should you begin an auction on eBay or Amazon? What day should you choose for it to end on? Buyers have real lives (typically) and are usually busy during the day with other things. Their free time tends to be in the evenings and on weekends. There is a three hour difference between one end of the United States and the other end. You want to make sure that the auction ends after 6:00 P.M. and before 10:00 P.M. for the whole country. Using eBay time (which is Pacific time), an ending time between 6:00 and 7:00 P.M. will allow most of your potential bidders to have a convenient access time. That means someone in the Central time zone, like me here in the Midwest, should place listings on eBay or Amazon between 8:00 and 9:00 P.M. Between 9:00 and 10:00 P.M. works well for the Eastern time zone. This strategy is for auctions ending on a weekday. For auctions ending on a weekend, you have greater flexibility. Traditionally, bidders are more likely to be home during the day on Sunday than on Saturday. A Sunday afternoon visit to eBay is fast becoming a cherished tradition in many households.

NOTE When you plan your ending times for auctions, consider time zones outside the continental United States, as well as international times. For example, when it is 7:00 P.M. in New York, it will be 2 P.M. in Hawaii and midnight in England.

How Long Should My Auction Last?

All of the Big Three auction sites let you choose from a range of days for the length of your auction. The default and traditional length of time for an auction is seven days. This works well for sellers who sit at their computers on Sunday afternoons, entering their new listings and watching their current auctions ending, or for sellers who start their work week on Mondays by reviewing their successes from the week before and waiting to launch a series of new auctions.

Here are possible reasons for choosing a longer auction:

- ◆ Your auction is aimed at a fairly small audience, and you want to give them time to find your auction.

- ◆ You won't be available to watch the end of the auction, notify winners quickly, and be around to fulfill your obligations in the few days after an auction ends, so you pick a different day for it to end on.

- ◆ Your schedule is such that it is more convenient for you to deal with the end of an auction on a certain day, and you time the auction to end on that day.

- ◆ You informed key bidders about your auction, and you want to give them ample opportunity to respond.

- ◆ You figure that the longer the auction lasts, the more bids you will get.

Here are reasons for choosing a shorter auction:

- ◆ You need money quickly.

- ◆ You advertise a quick-ending auction to create some attention and excitement among bidders.

- ◆ You have the time and energy to deal with several auctions opening and closing constantly.

- ◆ You are capitalizing on a very current and possibly extremely brief interest in your item. For example, a PBS special last night featured the turn-of-the-century magician Thurstone and the personalized cards he would fling to the crowd. You have one of these cards, and you hope to sell it quickly while it is still fresh in the memory of magic memorabilia collectors.

Using Software to Upload Listings

The software included in this book allows you to quickly upload auction listings to eBay. Additionally, all Big Three sites provide free *bulk loaders* (as they are called), which you can download from their sites.

> **NOTE** As mentioned throughout this book, some independent auction resource sites—like www.auctionwatch.com and auction.goto.com—provide many support services to sellers and buyers, including management of auction listings.

With Auction Wizard, you can click a button and go instantly to the eBay Sell Your Item page. All the fields will be filled in automatically for you, based on the information you already entered offline. Here's how:

1. From the Web Wizard window, click the List On eBay button.

2. When you are automatically connected to the Listing Entry eBay page, verify that all the fields have been entered with the correct information for the first item in your auction lot.

3. If the fields are correct, click the Submit My Listing button on the New Item Verification Page.

4. In Auction Wizard, click the Lot Is On Line button.

5. Click the Next Lot button, and repeat the listing process for the next item.

> **NOTE** When you use the software available with this book, or software you download from the auction sites, check for updates before you use them. Many functions are designed based on the current auction-site page designs. If the page designs change, your software may need to be updated. Such updating, if necessary, is usually free and is done over the Internet. Most software provides a Web location to find out about, and get updates.

Bulk Loaders

The Big Three sites provide free software downloads to help prepare several auction listings and upload them all at the same time.

eBay Mister Lister, eBay's easy-listing software, is available only to users with a feedback rating of 10 or higher. Find out about it, and begin downloading it at:

pages.ebay.com/services/buyandsell/composer-info.html

Yahoo!   Yahoo!'s bulk loader, Auction Express, is available for anyone (in exchange for a little survey information) at the following address:

`batch.auctions.yahoo.com/show/batchinquiry`

Amazon   Amazon's listing software is offered only to high-volume sellers. You can get started on your journey at:

`s1.amazon.com/exec/varzea/subst/selling/bulk/bulk-loading.html`

WARNING Amazon's Bulk Lister and Yahoo!'s Auction Express require a lot more setup work than eBay's Mister Lister. They work only in unison with other software, like spreadsheets.

Once you have Auction Wizard, or one of the other bulk loaders ready to go, creating your listings offline (a great option if your online access time is limited) and sending them to the sites is a simple matter. Here are the steps for uploading auctions on Mister Lister:

1. Start a new Collection.

2. Enter all the listing information, including item descriptions, for each auction and add them to the Collection.

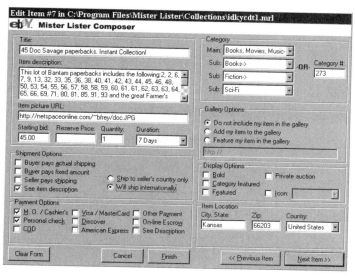

3. When you are ready, send the whole collection to eBay using the Send This Collection button.

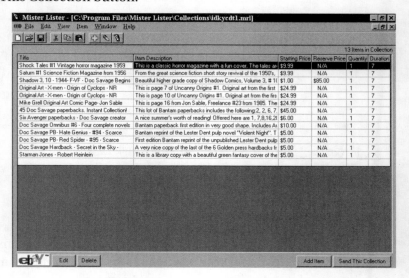

4. On eBay, you verify that the listings are correct and approve them. Your auctions will begin right away!

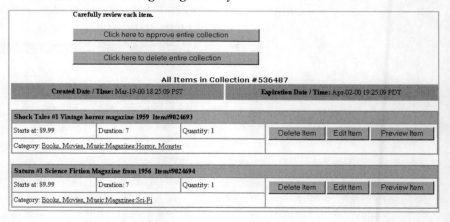

NOTE With Mister Lister, the first time you see the eBay page showing you all the auctions that await your approval, you may not see all of them. A brief delay is common, so refresh your screen a couple of times until they show up.

51 Expert Advice on Listings

Our panel of online auction know-it-alls have some thoughts about constructing a great listing.

User ID: xjhawkx
Category: Sports Cards

"A good listing needs to have a picture, detailed description of the item(s), and explain the shipping-and-return policy. Hide nothing and people will keep coming back. If you have multiple items listed, it is also a good idea to ask people to view your other similar items, and e-mail you with questions or special requests."

User UD: aaagh!
Category: Comic Book Art

"Offer something people want or something you can possibly convince people they want. Be clear—item title, item description, payment, and postage terms should be separated so as not to look confusing. Get a scanner or digital camera, both can be found for under $100, and practice to get good pictures of what you are selling. If you don't like the look of the pictures you take, no one else will either."

User ID: ssabellico
Category: Star Wars

"Be honest…but be creative. Be honest about the condition of your item. In these times of Mint in the Box, people are very particular about what THEY consider mint. If you're selling a poster, mention the small crease in the corner. If you're selling an opened action figure that still has the box, label it as a loose figure with box. Does the box have a price tag on it? Mention it. Does the box still have the twisty ties? Mention it. Does it have the cellophane that originally covered it? Mention it. It's always better to be up front

about what the product is like in the DESCRIPTION, rather than having the person receive it and realize it's not up to their standards—earning you a bad rating.

Another listing trick: Mention what the item is GOOD for. It you're selling a lot of action figures, mention that it is a 'good way to catch up on your collection.' If you're selling a bunch of Star Wars magazines, mention that they're 'read copies' and that its 'great reference material.' Another thing: find your niche. Those great Cinescape magazines with Star Wars on the cover? They're not just 'a great reference guide for the Star Wars fan,' but they're also 'a great reference guide for the Star Wars fan and budding filmmaker.'

Pictures, pictures, pictures. Find a way to get pictures on your listing. For one thing they're free. . . so it stands to reason that you're only harming yourself by NOT having one. Think about your own bids. What were the listings you checked? You can bet it was the listings with the pictures you checked first. If you don't want to invest in a scanner or digital camera, there are alternatives. Most people own a video camera, and there's a small device called Snappy that plugs into your printer port. Install the software, plug your video camera into Snappy, and you're ready to go. My $100 investment paid for itself with the numerous sales I made by having pictures with my auctions. Regarding pictures, make sure they look good. As much as a good picture will help you, a bad picture can harm you. Dimly lit, murky, muddy pictures subliminally turn people away. Again, look at how the pros do it. Open a magazine to a perfume ad. It's just a bottle usually, but it looks good."

Expert Summary

What is our panel saying here? They agree that a quality listing depends on a little salesmanship and a good picture. Give bidders the information they need, give them a reason to bid, and give them a good look at what you've got to sell!

Your Name on the Shingle

Creating a presence on the Web is a great opportunity to design who you are from scratch. Your persona is a blank slate, where you can create the kind of person you want to be. This portion of the book focuses on becoming the kind of seller you want to be.

You are free to become a grouchy, deceptive seller of low quality merchandise, or you can become a friendly, honest seller of really cool stuff! I'm pretty sure you want to reach the second goal, not the first, and the following tips are designed to help you reach that goal.

52   Deciding What to Sell

You may be eager to start or expand your online auction presence, but you may not be sure what junk—er…uh…I mean collectibles or useful products—to sell. With thousands of categories to choose from, how do you know which one is best for you? Here are some criteria to help you decide:

Sell What You Know   I know comic books, Doc Savage paraphernalia, and paperback books based on 1960s and 1970s TV shows, so that's what I sell. What do you know a lot about? Experience with a line of products is crucial for knowing a good price, how to identify and describe the item, being able to answer questions, and marketing to the concerns of likely buyers for your type of item. Dealing with stuff you like is also a lot of fun.

WARNING As a seller, avoid using these sorts of phrases:
"I don't know how to grade baseball cards, but this one looks in good shape to me."
"I don't usually sell bone china, but…."
If you are selling something you don't know much about, learn more about it. If you are buying, on the other hand, these phrases might mean trouble—or they might represent an opportunity to get a good deal.

Sell What You Have Too Much Of   Earlier, we defined a collectible as anything you have more of than you need. Online auctions are a great opportunity to sell used stuff that still has value, but that you don't need or want. They are also a way to get rid of anything you have extra copies of (for example, books, music, and clothes). When you get tired of that toy or video game or electronic gizmo, you have more than you need of it, so sell it!

Sell What You Can Make Money From   We have talked about different ways to define profit. If you plan to make online auction selling a business, you've got to specialize in selling items from which you can make a lot of money. If you can find a reliable source for a good product at a low cost to you (maybe a wholesale dealer or a regular drive to Saturday morning estate sales), consider making that product your primary line.

Sell What's Rare   The key to big profits is low supply and high demand. If you sell the same thing as every other Tom, Dick, and Harry, there will be high supply. Search out the unique, the one-of-a-kinds, and become a master of selling those things that no one has ever seen before. Some categories contain almost nothing but unique items—art, memorabilia, and so on.

Sell What People Will Buy   Technically, I suppose it is impossible to sell something that people won't buy, but you can try awfully hard to sell something no one wants. If you have some options and can sell a variety of things, explore the listings by category at Amazon, Yahoo!, and eBay. Which categories have the most auctions, and more importantly, which categories have the most successful auctions? Just the number of listings in a category, while not a perfect measure of the quantity of sales (because not all listings result in sales), is a good, rough estimate of where the action is. Table 52.1 lists the eBay categories with the most listings (found on a recent visit), the number of current auctions, and what that number is as a percentage of all auctions on eBay. You can treat this percentage as an index of the popularity of a category. With so many different categories and auctions listed, even the most popular category, Sports: Trading Cards, accounts for only about 7% of all auctions.

TABLE 52.1 Most Popular eBay Categories

eBay Category	Number of Current Auctions	Percent of All eBay Auctions
Sports: Trading Cards	330,000+	7.10
Music	250,000+	5.30
Books	240,000+	5.11
Memorabilia (Movies, TV, Music)	160,000+	3.40
Jewelry	140,000+	3.04
Sports: Memorabilia	130,000+	2.78
Movies	128,000+	2.75
Clothing: Women	108,000+	2.31
Stamps	100,000+	2.15
Collectibles: Advertising	98,000+	2.10
Collectibles: Paper	95,000+	2.03
Glass	91,000+	1.95
Toys: Diecast	86,000+	1.85
Pottery	82,000+	1.76
Porcelain	81,000+	1.74
Toys: Bean Bag Plush	78,000+	1.67
Automotive	75,000+	1.61
Computers: Hardware	75,000+	1.59
Sports: Sporting Goods	73,000+	1.57
Comic Books	60,000+	1.29
Consumer Electronics	60,000+	1.29

TABLE 52.1 Most Popular eBay Categories (Continued)

eBay Category	Number of Current Auctions	Percent of All eBay Auctions
Magazines	58,000+	1.24
Toys: Action Figures	57,000+	1.23
Coins: US	52,000+	1.11
Toys: Games	51,000+	1.10

Onsite Support for Sellers

Along with various links, discussion boards, and FAQ pages at eBay, Yahoo!, and Amazon, you will find two additional modes of support for sellers:

◆ Store Fronts

◆ Selling Tools and Resources

Store Fronts are do-it-yourself home pages that reside on the auction site's server. They organize a seller's auctions, provides links and information about the seller, and to some degree establish a more well-rounded identity for users.

On eBay, the About Me page serves as the Store Front. (To build your own, choose About Me from the Services menu at the top of every page.) You can choose from three types of layouts, write about yourself or your policies (including HTML formatting), show your current auctions and recent feedback, and include a photo of yourself (or your goldfish, I suppose). Yahoo!, in addition to its own minimal About Me profiles that all Yahoo! users can establish, has Auction Booths, which we talked about earlier. Yahoo! Auction Booths provide display and formatting options similar to eBay's. They also provide the option to easily include a personalized logo that you have created elsewhere.

On Amazon, choose Your Account and Seller Account from any page to see your Store Front options. My Storefronts, or *zShops,* are Amazon-based display pages for any sellers on Amazon, not just auction sellers. This page acts almost as a stand-alone Web store. It includes a search engine which searches only through the seller's current list of items for sale or auction, as well as the usual space for photos, links, and information. In addition to, or instead of zShops, Amazon auctioneers can build an Auctions About Me page which includes information, a link to their homepage, and room for a logo.

We've already talked about bulk listing software available for free at the Big Three sites. In addition, the sites provide a variety of tools and other support for power sellers and those who want to be power sellers.

Clicking on the Auction Seller Success link on Amazon's Seller Account page will make available a selection of Seller's Tools for Success. Among other resources, you can activate Merchant Tools, which provides great flexibility in searching and displaying your current, past, and future auctions, and allows for efficient downloading of auction information.

Yahoo! Auctions has fewer auction-specific resources than the other two sites—though the massive Yahoo! site in its entirety is certainly a valuable business resource—and we have already talked about their bulk loader for listings. For now, you can start at the Options page (through a link at the top of every Auction page), and sign up to subscribe to a Yahoo! Auctions e-mail newsletter.

NOTE Remember, number 49, "Sending Them to Your Web Site and Other HTML Tricks" lets you know how to include a link in your auctions which will send potential buyers from your auctions to your personal homepage.

53 Tracking the Competition

It pays to know what the competition is up to. You can learn from them, check to see what prices similar items are selling for, and educate yourself on how unique your product truly is. In some respects, I suppose, your competition is all the other millions of sellers on your auction site, but there is plenty of room out there and life is a lot easier if you don't assume that everybody else is out to get you. Let's treat competition as an opportunity to learn and improve our own business. Here's how to keep tabs on the store across the street:

Even if you are auctioning an absolutely one-of-a-kind item, you have competition. Someone is selling something similar—similar in type or function, or similar in just-how-cool-it-would-be-to-own. Knowing how much those similar items sell for would be useful information to have. A variety of systems could be used to get an up-to-date average of the current winning bid prices being realized by the competition. You know your own selling prices from the past, of course, but here is a simple, fairly scientific and statistically sound method for estimating the current market price for items like yours. This system is a simple one, meaning that it is easy to apply and it only takes into account a couple of variables: the type of item sold and what it sold for. A more accurate system would require keeping track of many more variables: the type of auction, the number of similar items offered, the length of the auction, and so on. This is a quick-and-dirty method which provides an informed guess with minimum work.

1. Identify your *population* of similar items. A population is the whole group of items you are interested in describing. You won't gather information on this whole group, but you will choose a sample of items to gather information about. Define your population accurately, so you can be sure your sample fairly represents it.

2. On your auction site of choice (I'll assume eBay for this example because of the huge number of items in any given population), use the site to create pages of listings of completed auctions in your population. If your defined population, or list of items for sale, is also a category, then doing this is pretty easy. If your defined population is more specific than a category, then use the results of a search that defines your population. Experiment until you can generate an on-screen list of all completed auctions that match your population.

3. If there are so few members of your population of items that you can easily record the winning bid of every auction, then do that; otherwise, you will have to randomly choose a sample of completed auctions for your information. You can randomly choose by checking every second or third or fourth auction on each page. If there are

dozens of pages of completed auctions in your population, then just use every second or third or fourth page.

4. Average the winning bids, and you'll have a pretty decent and easily obtained guess of what your item is worth in the current environment. The more closely your population resembles the item you are selling, the more precise this method will be. Make sure you are comparing apples with apples and not with oranges.

An even more accurate use of this information comes when you sample auctions on a regular basis over time and can identify trends. Are prices rising or falling?

Here are some things you can watch for and learn from:

◆ If you can identify a few primary competitors, learn from them. Check their feedback on a regular basis. What do their customers say about them. What do their customers like about the way they do business?

◆ If your competitors sell a unique product that they produce themselves, like auction software or CDs full of get-rich-quick tools, buy a copy and learn from it.

◆ Bookmarking your major competitor's Current Auctions By page can pay off. This will provide a quick snapshot of what they are selling and what bids they are getting.

◆ If you are a large seller, identify your competition. Check their Web site for their retail selling prices, estimate the most they will pay for stuff, and then outbid them.

54 Setting Sales Policies

We have already looked at some ways to help you decide what rules you should enforce during transactions. There are site policies, which you should follow, and there are laws which you should follow; but beyond that, you have the freedom to choose almost any sales policy you want. We have already talked in detail about some specific procedures and philosophies you can adopt to help yourself or to help the customer (like feedback policies and communication policies). This chapter presents a more generalized method which can be useful in shaping policy. The method can be called the Yes-Yes method, the Win-Win method, or the Everyone's Happy method.

This method is based on the fact that every sales policy will benefit the seller, the buyer, both, or neither. The single assumption is that there is a proper hierarchy in deciding which choice among a set of alternatives is the best policy. The best policy benefits both the seller and the buyer. The second best policy benefits the buyer. The third best policy benefits the seller. The worst policy benefits neither. This method obviously prioritizes the customer's benefit over the seller's.

NOTE The benefit I am talking about here is an immediate benefit. What is easiest? What takes the least work? We would probably agree that if a policy benefits a buyer, then eventually the seller will benefit as well, through increased sales, good reputation, and so on. That kind of delayed, long-term benefit is not the kind used in the Yes-Yes method, though a proper application of the method will benefit the seller, of course, and that is its purpose.

Let's apply the method to some online auction policy options and see how it might work, as shown in Tables 54.1, 54.2, and 54.3.

TABLE 54.1 How Much Should A Seller Charge for Postage and Handling?

Policy	Benefits the Seller?	Benefits the Buyer?
Seller always charges the same amount, regardless of the true mailing cost.	Sometimes. If True, postage cost is less than the charge.	Sometimes. If True, postage cost is more than the charge.
Seller charges more than the mailing cost to cover other expenses.	Yes. Increased profit.	No. Extra cost.

TABLE 54.1 How Much Should A Seller Charge for Postage and Handling? (Continued)

Policy	Benefits the Seller?	Benefits the Buyer?
Seller charges less than the mailing cost to help the buyer.	No. Lost profit.	Yes. Money saved.
Seller charges the exact mailing costs.	Yes. No lost profit.	Yes. No extra cost.

The double "Yes" tells us that the best policy is to charge the exact cost for postage and handling. Is this worth the trouble of exchanging a couple of extra e-mails to find out the buyer's location and report back to them how much to add in postage? The method suggests it is worth the time.

NOTE Although I recommend that sellers charge exact shipping costs, some high volume sellers suggest a different approach. To minimize the number of e-mail exchanges, some sellers charge a flat fee for domestic shipping and a flat fee for international shipping. They choose a fee that is high enough to cover typical costs regardless of destination. The seller may make a little sometimes, lose a little other times, and expects things to even out in the end.

TABLE 54.2 What Sort of E-mail Should a Seller Send to Confirm a Winning Bid?

Policy	Benefits the Seller?	Benefits the Buyer?
Seller waits for the winning bidder to send an e-mail.	No. Sale is delayed or never happens.	No. Purchase is delayed or never happens.
Seller sends a generic e-mail which does not include the bidder's name (User ID) or the amount of the winning bid.	Yes. Requires little effort.	No. Must go online and check listing for information.

TABLE 54.2   What Sort of E-mail Should a Seller Send to Confirm a Winning Bid? (Continued)

Policy	Benefits the Seller?	Benefits the Buyer?
Seller sends an e-mail which refers to the item only by the item number, not by title.	Yes. Helps seller with record-keeping.	No. Must go online to verify which auction they won.
Seller sends an e-mail which is personalized to them (by User ID), gives the winning bid and postage information (if known).	No. It is more work, requires software or both.	Yes. Provides buyer with personalized note and relevant information.
Seller forwards the e-mail received from the auction site, adding pleasantries and payment information.	Yes. Very little work required.	Yes. Provides all necessary information.

This time, the double "Yes" suggests a policy that is easy for the seller and benefits the buyer. Good customer service is sometimes also the easiest thing to do!

NOTE If you find that you are including much of the same text in all the e-mails you send, you can automate a lot of the process without turning to specialized software. Create a text document with the commonly used text, and copy and paste into new e-mails. Another option is to use the Send Again feature you may have on your e-mail software, and send the same e-mail each time (changing the recipient and relevant auction info).

TABLE 54.3   Should a Seller Offer a Money-Back Guarantee?

Policy	Benefits the Seller?	Benefits the Buyer?
Seller does not offer a money-back guarantee.	Yes. All sales are final.	No. All sales are final.
Seller offers a money-back guarantee, but only if the item is not as described.	No. May lose sales.	Yes. Small protection.

TABLE 54.3 Should a Seller Offer a Money-Back Guarantee? (Continued)

Policy	Benefits the Seller?	Benefits the Buyer?
Seller offers an unconditional five-day money-back guarantee.	No. May lose sales.	Yes. Some protection.
Seller offers an unconditional two-week money back guarantee.	No. May lose sales.	Yes. Plenty of time to receive and examine the item.

In this example, we have three policies from which to choose. Although there aren't any Yes-Yes situations, there are three policies that benefit the buyer. The choosing rule here might be to pick the policy that benefits the buyer most, which, in this case, would seem to be the two-week unconditional money-back guarantee.

What if a policy benefits the buyer, but hurts you, the seller? If a policy hurts you too much (for example, you lose money or the workload is too high), don't choose it, regardless of the benefit to the buyer.

If you have trouble deciding which way to go with a policy choice, try the Yes-Yes method. List all possible policy choices you are considering and see if one of them benefits both you and the customer. If you see a double "Yes," you have your answer.

55 Privacy Policies

As a member of the growing Web community, you have the opportunity and obligation to help establish what is acceptable and what is proper when it comes to privacy. In its broadest sense, privacy on the Net covers everything from the proper storage and use of identifying information about your buyers and your sellers to using someone's real name in public feedback to collecting bidder's e-mail addresses to looking up a user's street address to sharing e-mail messages. Auction site policies enforce what you can and cannot do on any given site, and we discuss those elsewhere. However, beyond site policy, every business has the obligation to develop its own policy with regard to this issue. To see how privacy impacts your policies regardless of the size of your online presence, consider the following scenarios—all based on actual online experiences, some of which are fairly common:

1. You are bidding on an important painting. You receive an e-mail from someone claiming to be the artist's son who states that the item is stolen and informs you that if you win the auction you will be purchasing stolen property. Later, the seller contacts you and other bidders who received the warning letter and denies the allegations and needs copies of the e-mail you received from the artist's son as evidence of libel. Should you provide a copy?

2. You haven't received payment yet from a winning bidder. You haven't sent the item, yet. Your e-mails go unanswered, though the bidder did respond to your first notification. The auction site allows you to look up a user's address, including their real name. With this information, you can search the Web and get a phone number. Should you use this process and get the phone number, so you can call and make sure the bidder still wants the item?

3. You sell Beanie Babies. A company contacts you and offers to buy your list of e-mail addresses, real names, and addresses of Beanie buyers. Should you sell?

4. You discover that two user IDs have the same mailing address. One ID has good feedback, the other does not. Should you let Amazon know about this trick? Is it even a trick?

There aren't obvious moral Yes or No answers to most of these questions.

However, site policies provide clear ethical guidance on Scenario 3. Selling e-mail addresses is not allowed.

Site policies provide less clear guidance on Scenario 1. Providing copies of e-mail might be considered releasing private user information (which can't be done without permission) On the other hand, the first e-mail was sent to you without solicitation.

As for Scenario 2, you may access user information to verify identity and to pursue post-auction obligations, like payment from a winning bidder.

As you try to answer these and other questions for yourself, you should try to build a consistent set of rules, some criteria you can use to answer them. Eventually, you may notice a philosophy. And that philosophy can become your policy. Your policy should be consistent with site policy (after all, you are choosing to do business there), but your policy can go beyond site policy in reach and in specifics.

Many consumer advocacy groups have put forth standards for privacy policies which protect and support the consumer. Because customer service is the prime source of most of the online auction selling strategies we've discussed, the perspective of these groups is useful to consider. Here are some examples of policies for any Internet-based business and what the impact of adopting each policy might be on you:

◆ Information about customers should not be released to anyone without prior permission or court order. (Would this policy allow you to display copies of e-mail from satisfied customers?)

◆ Information collected to fill orders should be deleted after a few months. (Would this policy allow you to build e-mailing lists to advertise your current auctions or send catalogs, even with an "opt-in" requirement?)

◆ Credit card transactions should be processed through encryption services. (Would this policy allow you to encourage buyers to e-mail you their credit card information?)

◆ Do not collect personal information from children. (Is it possible to sell to any child online without collecting personal information about them?)

The key to developing your own privacy policy is to first be aware of the issues, and then to build a policy that benefits the buyer. Businesses that make policy decisions based on what helps the customer are following a winning strategy.

56 Is a Ruble Worth More than a Flintstone?

At first thought, it might not sound like it is worth it to sell to bidders outside of the United States. You may be worried about the cost of mailing, the language barriers, or the amount of time it takes to mail back and forth. Don't let these concerns stop you from opening your auctions up to the five or six billion potential bidders who don't happen to live nearby. Although postage will cost more, you can charge the buyer for the additional cost. The buyer knew enough English to sign up on the auction site and bid on your item. Although the package will take longer to arrive at its destination, the wait will be worth it! Go ahead and check the Will Ship Internationally box when you post your auction. Here's some more information on issues of international selling:

Exchange Rates and Currencies   The official currency for the Big Three online auction sites is the American dollar, so it is reasonable for you to require, and the assumption will be, that all payments are made in U. S. dollars. The seller and the buyer, though, can agree to use any country's currency if they want. You may have noticed auctions with amounts listed in British pounds and, regardless of site policy, these sellers may have grown to expect payment in that currency. In most cases, unless they are very new to online auctions, their policy will be stated. Exchange rates can be calculated at the Universal Currency Converter on the Web at `www.xe.net/ucc/full.shtml`.

NOTE Providing exchange rate information can be a nice customer service you provide to international bidders, to help them get a sense of how much the current bid is in their currency.

Delivery Time   By air, packages still take only a few days to get to the farthest points on Earth, but by land the trip can be more than a month. If a buyer is willing to pay the extra postage for the cost of a plane, you can promise quick delivery. Air shipment is not *always* more expensive than land, but the cost is frequently substantially more—so you and your customers should probably just accept the reality of a long waiting time between payment and delivery. As we discussed previously, Federal Express and Airborne Express will ship internationally and you can check with them for exact costs and delivery times.

Customs   When products are sent to other countries, they must clear customs. Some countries charge a fee for that service. If a country does charge for customs, the buyer is expected to pay that fee. Packages sent to other nations require a signed customs form which identifies the contents and their value. Here are some Web sources for more information on custom requirements when selling internationally:

United States Customs Service   www.customs.ustreas.gov

Canada Customs and Revenues Agency   www.ccra-adrc.gc.ca

World Customs Organization   www.wcoomd.org

NOTE   Although Amazon encourages international sales, its A-to-Z Guarantee, which covers transactions, applies only to American, British, or German auctions.

Perhaps your first consideration when planning for international sales is whether to sell internationally at all. Some experienced sellers avoid the hassle altogether and have a stated policy of selling only to United States residents or, perhaps, U. S. or Canadian residents. They feel that the added complexities of dealing with international shipping, language conflicts, time delays, and postage costs are not worth the benefits of a few extra potential bidders. Let your own experiences guide you on this issue.

57 Expert Customer Service Advice

Our panel of thoughtful sellers agree on the importance of customer service.

User ID: ssabellico
Category: Star Wars

"Be prompt and courteous. Remember, online auctions are a business and should be run as such. This isn't a fanboy who just bid in your auction, it's a paying customer. Once the bidding is over, contact your winner right away. Be friendly, but professional. Make them feel special. Congratulate them on their win.

Personalize your e-mail to them. There's nothing worse than getting a form letter e-mail that just says 'send your money to this address, and don't send cash….' Be specific in your e-mail. Don't expect your customers to remember the shipping and winning bid. Detail everything in the e-mail. What was the item? How much was the final bid? How much was shipping? How much are those added together? What form of payment do you accept? How soon should they send it? How soon should they expect their package to arrive?

Pack your items as if they're going to be thrown from a moving truck. Put plenty of packing material around the sides. Again, in the age of Mint in the Box, it would be a shame to lose a sale because the mint item was damaged in shipping. Send an e-mail letting your customer know that the item is in the mail. In the e-mail, ask them to send you an e-mail when they receive it and POST A RATING. Ratings are what make more sales. Think about it. . . would you bid on an item from someone who has 50 ratings—25 of them bad? Don't badger your customer about ratings, but make it clear that you would like one if they are satisfied with their transaction."

User ID: aaagh
Category: Comic Book Art

"Don't argue with customers, offer a refund to anyone who wants one (especially if there is something wrong with the product you sold). But set restrictions, like when you request payment, give as exact a time as possible for delivery, and set out the procedure for items lost or damaged in the post. Basically, treat customers as you'd want to be treated. It's easy."

User ID: xjhawkx
Category: Sports Cards

"Getting a bad reputation is meaningless for a buyer, but it spells death to a seller. Disputes about transactions usually center on the condition of the item and that is why a detailed description is very important. Make sure the buyer knows the item as if they were standing in front of you holding it. Do not hide anything. And if the buyer insists on getting their money back, let them do it. Chances are you can sell the same item to someone else for about the same price. Communicate clearly and as often as needed to ensure a worry-free and smooth transaction."

Expert Summary

Our regular-people experts all feel that quality communication is the key to great customer service. Clear, prompt, and most importantly, friendly responses to inquiries and concerns greatly decrease the chances of a transaction-gone-wrong. Not only is life better when everyone is courteous to each other, but business will be better, too!

More Expert Advice on Customer Service

An amazing reference work of legendary status in my world of comic books is *The Photo-Journal Guide to Comic Books* by Ernst and Mary Gerber, published in 1990 by Gerber Publishing Company. The Gerbers present photos of almost all important comic books of the twentieth century and provide invaluable data on their true scarcity today. The advice they give regarding how to treat customers if you are in the auction business, as the Gerbers have been for decades, is important and it applies to our current discussion.

The book provides the following guidelines for how to behave as a quality seller in the auction business:

◆ Selling is an art. It takes some skill, some patience, and improves with practice.

◆ Test the waters before plunging in. A common mistake is to assume that selling your particular type of item is no different than selling anything else. What you sell is different than whatever anyone else sells, and you have to learn the specific ins-and-outs of your business.

◆ Be reliable.

◆ Behave consistently.

◆ Do what you have promised you will do.

◆ Allow customers to use credit cards.

◆ Work hard.

Selling into the
Online
Community

Our final discussion will focus on your community responsibilities as a seller. We've discussed the role a *citizen* of the Web plays in online auctions as a buyer, and now it's time to think about the obligations of a seller. Yahoo!, eBay, and Amazon have community spirit. Anyone, like you, who has spent time on these auction sites knows what I mean. It is an interactive, overwhelmingly friendly experience. Citizens rely on each other to play fair, be nice, and help others. (Not coincidentally, those are the same responsibilities my neighbors expect of me in the town where I live.) Sellers, like everyone else, want to fit in and contribute, and you can do that by following the rules and learning from your neighbors.

58   Following the Rules

Amazon, Yahoo!, and eBay have fairly long lists of rules and regulations. They were developed through common sense, experience, and concerns for user privacy and other rights. You should read through the list on the site you are using. In fact, before getting access to these sites, you had to click a button signifying that you agreed to follow the rules, so you should at least know what you agreed to. I won't list all the rules, but I will highlight the more important and most relevant ones. There is considerable overlap of policies among the three sites; what is required at one site is likely required at the others. If you break the rules and someone complains, or if you break the rules and the site discovers it, you will be warned or suspended, at the least, and permanently kicked out, at the worst. Many of the site policies are also the law of the land, so even worse consequences may await you. My guess, though, is that you are concerned about the right way to sell at online auctions and you aren't the unethical type (unless you stole this book, I guess). Here are some highlights of the site guidelines, many of which you might not have thought about. Some are specific to eBay, which has the most detailed policy, and Amazon (because Yahoo! doesn't charge, they have fewer rules), but you should follow these guidelines regardless of the site you are on.

NOTE To be specific, the typical pattern of punishment after infractions is: 1. Warning, 2. 30-day suspension, 3. Second Warning, and 4. Expulsion.

All Users

The following rules apply to all users:

◆ You may not interfere with other bidder's or seller's activities.

◆ You may not manipulate bidding.

Buyers

The following rules apply to all buyers:

◆ You must honor a winning bid.

◆ You do not have to honor a non-winning bid (for example, you were the second-highest bidder, but the winning bidder cannot be contacted).

◆ You may retract a bid only in extreme circumstances (for example, you mistype your bid amount or you have reasonable suspicions about a seller's identity) or if the seller changes the description of an item.

◆ When you bid, you are bound to pay the additional costs described in the listing.

◆ Only adults may bid on items in an Adult category.

Sellers

The following rules apply to all sellers:

◆ Items should be in the appropriate category.

◆ Dutch auctions must be comprised of the same type of items.

◆ You must honor winning bids except under extreme circumstances (for example, you cannot verify the buyer's identity or they do not honor their bidder obligations).

◆ Your listings may not link to other auction sites or to sites where similar items are being sold at less than your minimum bid amount.

◆ You may not offer a low, minimum starting bid, but charge the real price as an unreasonably high "shipping" cost.

◆ You may not have an e-mail address or Web site name in your listing title.

◆ In your description, you may not offer a single item and indicate that additional items are available at the same price.

◆ You may not use site-collected e-mail addresses to send unsolicited commercial messages.

◆ You may not sell alcohol, animals, drugs, firearms, fireworks, human parts or remains, postage meters, stocks, or tobacco.

N O T E   Recently, a young man was in the news for having "sold his soul" on eBay for $5. (He got the idea from a storyline on the television show *The Simpsons*.) The wise judges at eBay conferred and determined that the sale was not allowable. Their thinking was that there were two possibilities: 1. The human soul does not exist, in which case the sale was fraudulent, or 2. The soul does exist, in which case it is a human body part and cannot be sold on eBay. In either case, the auction was a site violation. You can't argue with that logic!

eBay Social Support

A variety of groups, programs, and organized Help pages on eBay have the sole purpose of protecting the online community and ensuring a pleasant place to hang out. We've discussed SafeHarbor, eBay's site safety and protection resource, several times in this book. SafeHarbor has specific categories of assistance, as well as other social support systems, available:

◆ Message boards (areas for posted discussion among members) exist on a variety of special topics: HTML, photos, international trading, technical issues, and so on. Start learning from other users at `pages.ebay.com/community/chat/index.html`.

- You can sign up for the free eBay Insider e-mail newsletter, which provides tips, news, anecdotes, and such. Start with the back issues at `pages.ebay.com/community/life/ebay-life-pA1.html`.

- You can join Usenet discussion boards, which are run independently of eBay. The Usenet topic is `alt.marketing.online.ebay`. If you do your Usenet group browsing through the portal Remarq at `www.remarq.com`, the discussion threads will include the eBay discussion boards.

- To report suspicious or illegal trading activity, e-mail eBay at `safe-harbor@ebay.com`. Before sending your complaint, start by learning more about this process at `pages.ebay.com/help/community/investigates.html`.

- For information and links about pursuing your options when sales are not completed and you suspect fraud, start at `pages.ebay.com/help/community/insurance.html`.

- The Community Watch department is concerned with the sale of items that violate site policy. Start at `cgi3.ebay.com/aw-cgi/eBayISAPI.dll?ReportInfringing` to report a violation and learn more about the topic at `pages.ebay.com/help/community/png-items.html`.

- The Verified Rights Owner Program (VeRO) is an eBay system to protect the rights of owners of intellectual property. Intellectual property includes patents, trademarks, and copyrighted material. Owners of such material who discover unauthorized auctions selling their intellectual property, or selling items that infringe on their property rights, are encouraged to join VeRO by filling out some forms (available at `pages.ebay.com/help/community/notice-infringe2.pdf`) identifying the auction numbers and the specific infringement.

NOTE Although eBay will quickly investigate complaints or charges about unfair trading practices, they will not investigate most complaints about feedback, refusal of sellers or buyers to honor winning bids, or the perfectly legal (but sometimes irritating to other bidders) practice of sniping.

59 Learning from Your Customers

If you sell collectibles, your customers benefit you in ways other than the green, easily stored money they send. You benefit by sharing your love for your hobby, your interest in cool, unique and/or historic stuff, and by making people happy. You can also learn from those who respond to your auctions. You can learn details about your world of collecting (helping to make you even more of a super-smart expert than you are now), and you can learn more about the business of selling (making you even more of a super-smart seller than you are now).

Learning about Your Hobby

Here are just a few ways you will learn more about your field by listening to your customers:

They will e-mail you with corrections. When you make a mistake in your item description, or use the wrong terminology, you will probably get a friendly correction. You will quickly learn the right words to use to describe your Queen Anne chair (the one you've been mistakenly describing as a Queen Jan chair), or you will be reminded that the VIC-20 computer system you have up for auction is probably not "brand new."

They will suggest better categories. A movie poster is not original art, even if it is an original poster, and a Jimmy Carter statuette doesn't belong in the Mr. Peanut category.

They will answer your questions. Your listing description can include friendly "asides" that solicit information. If you are selling a videotape of the movie *I Married a Monster from Outer Space*, you can say "One of director Gene Fowler, Jr.'s best horror films. Are his other films available on tape? I've never seen them offered." Quick as a whip, you will probably get a response to your question—along with, hopefully, a bid or two. When you ship the item or e-mail confirmation of a winning bid, you can ask the winning bidder why they are interested in the item you are selling, and you might learn a ton more.

Buyers can become great trading partners and story-swappers. I've developed nice friends and sources of information over the years from online auction users I have bought from or sold to. You can gather buddies online and build a network of those who share your enthusiasm for old radio shows or the mystery novels of Agatha Christie or Dungeons and Dragons rule books or Beatles memorabilia.

Learning to Be a Better Seller

A good seller often needs to be a good listener.

Successful sellers always want to improve and do a better job of meeting their customer's needs and expectations. The best way to do that is to simply listen to them. What are they telling you?

- ◆ Do you get complaints or returns because of the packaging you have chosen? Clearly your customers are telling you to package better.

- ◆ Do you get complaints or returns because the condition of the item was a disappointment to the buyer? Maybe you need some more practice or training to learn how to grade what you sell. Maybe you need to give more details about condition in your item descriptions.

- ◆ Do your buyers question the amount you charge for mailing? Maybe you need to explain that you include insurance in all transactions.

- ◆ Are you getting no bids? Your non-customers are telling you that they either don't want what you are selling or they won't pay the amount you are charging.

- ◆ Are your bids being retracted by the buyers? Maybe your item descriptions aren't clear on first reading or somehow are unintentionally deceptive.

- ◆ Are you getting negative feedback? The message here should be pretty clear and will be spelled out explicitly in the feedback comments.

- ◆ Are you getting no feedback at all? Your customers are telling you that they don't feel obligated to leave any. Should you ask for feedback?

- ◆ Are you getting e-mails asking for the status of transactions? Maybe you are being told to speed up your mailing time or increase the frequency of communication with buyers.

I once worked in a video store, many moons ago, and we required all sorts of information before we allowed customers to rent videos. When first-time customers complained about all the personal information we were asking them, what we heard was "I'm not very cooperative. I will be a bad customer." What they were actually saying, of course, was "Why are you making it hard for me to become a customer? You are driving me away!" It wasn't until we stopped pretending to listen and actually *listened* to what they were saying, that we changed our policies to make it easier on customers. With online auctions, treat the feedback and e-mails as literal statements of what your customers are saying to you. Listen to them. They probably know best.

60 Collectibles Certification Services

Some organizations and private companies have been established which help ensure the accurate description of items in certain collectibles areas. They provide some level of protection and assurance to communities of collectors. Many sellers in these areas report that "certified" items sell more easily and for higher prices than "non-certified" items—although it depends greatly on the specific customs of each collecting area. These services judge the condition and, in some cases, the authenticity of popular collectibles for a fee. Typically, they provide a field-accepted rating and a description of the condition of an item and then seal the item to ensure that its condition remains unchanged. Table 60.1 provides a sampling of these services.

TABLE 60.1 Certification Services

Collectible	Service	Web Site
Trading Cards	Professional Sports Authenticator	www.collectors.com/psa

TABLE 60.1 Certification Services (Continued)

Collectible	Service	Web Site
Stamps	**Professional Stamps Experts**	www.collectors.com/pse
Coins	**Professional Coin Grading Service**	www.collectors.com/pcgs
Comic Books	**Comics Guarantee**	www.cgccomics.com
Sports Autographs	**Online Authentics**	www.onlineauthentics.com

61 Online Sites and Organizations

A ton of groups and Web sites, outside of the online auction sites themselves, exist to discuss issues, educate, and build community. Here are just some of the independent sites and organizations you can become involved with to grow as an online auction professional:

Auction Insights   A collection of tips and opinions at www.auctioninsights.com.

Auction Patrol   Provides instruction, links, and support at www.auctionpatrol.com.

Auction Row   An auction search engine and software links at www.auctionrow.com.

Auction Tribune   An online auction newspaper at www.auctiontribune.com.

Auction Watch   A comprehensive collection of buyer and seller services and up-to-date news at www.auctionwatch.com.

Bidder's Edge   At www.biddersedge.com, you'll find some powerful auction search tools, notification services, and other auction tools to make your life easier.

Gomez.com Among other shopping resources is an updated quality ranking of auction sites at `www.gomez.com`.

GoTo.com Auctions Along with written advice and resources, this site provides an eBay authorized search engine to search many auction sites at one time at `www.auctions.goto.com`.

Online Auction Users Association An organization for small sellers and buyers to discuss issues, learn, and establish ethical codes of conduct at `www.auctionusers.org`.

Online Traders Web Alliance A clearinghouse of auction information, tools and discussion at `www.otwa.com`.

62 Reviewing for the Final Exam

I've presented some opinions here, along with some facts. We've discussed the strategies for becoming a winning bidder and the strategies for becoming a winning seller. The three online auction sites we looked at provide worlds of opportunity and fun, ways to make money, ways to spend money, ways to increase your collection, and ways to increase your business. You get to choose how you want to use online auction sites, and you get to decide your goals. Hopefully, this book will help you to reach those goals.

This final review summarizes the main points we covered. By now, they should sound at least familiar:

◆ Use the software that comes with this book. As a buyer, you will gain the advantage over others. As a seller, you will find the organizational tools and listing design aids invaluable.

◆ When bidding, enter a maximum bid which is exactly—to the penny—the most you are willing to pay. Consider sniping. There are greater benefits to bidding near the end of the auction than near the beginning—especially when you have the software to make it easy.

◆ Check the feedback of sellers before bidding.

◆ As a seller, always treat your customers with kindness and with respect. Avoid conflict.

◆ Listing descriptions should be as simple as possible, while still providing all necessary information. Use HTML commands to format your listing the way you want, but don't get carried away and lose the message among the flash.

◆ Always include a picture. If your product doesn't show up on film (like Dracula), include a graphic illustration.

◆ Think twice before using a reserve auction format, even one with a low reserve. Consider formats that increase impulse bidding, like those with low starting bids.

◆ Always list on eBay, as your first choice, because of their massive number of users, but use Yahoo! and Amazon too. Expanding your presence can only increase your chances for a successful sale. Amazon's ability to bring in customers from their retail site is potentially useful.

◆ Practice, practice, practice. Start slow and find your pace.

Good luck. Have fun. Next time you are at an online auction, give me a wave when you see me, and if you and I are both bidding on the same 1933 first issue of the Doc Savage pulp magazine (rarely offered), then look out. You are in for the fight of your life!

Online Auction Sites

All the sites on this list let the public buy and sell and they have a variety of auction categories.

321Gone	www.321gone.com
AcuBid.com	www.acubid.com
Amazon	www.amazon.com
America's Auctions and Sales	www.aaands.com
Auction 1 Online	www.auction1online.com
Auction Port	www.auctionport.com
Auction US	www.auctionus.com
Auction-Warehouse.com	www.auction-warehouse.com
Auctionaddict.com	www.auctionaddict.com
AuctionBuy	www.auctionbuy.com
AuctionFun.com	www.auctionfun.com
Auctions.com	www.auctions.com
Auctionscape	www.auctionscape.com
Barter-n-Trade	www.barter-n-trade.com
Bid Now	www.bidnow.com
Boxlot.com	www.boxplot.com
BuySell.net	www.buysell.net
Cutebid.com	www.cutebid.com
Cyber Auctions	www.cyber-auctions.com
eBay	www.ebay.com
edeal	www.edeal.com
Haggle Online	www.haggle.com

icollector	www.icollector.com
OnlineAuction.com	www.onlineauction.com
Sell and Trade	www.sellandtrade.com
Sellers Free Auction	www.sellersfreeauction.com
SoldUSA.com	www.soldusa.com
Tbay Auctions	www.tbayauctions.com
Yahoo!	www.yahoo.com

INDEX

• • • • • • • • • • • • • •

Note to the Reader: Page numbers in **bold** indicate the principal discussion of a topic or the definition of a term. Page numbers in *italic* indicate illustrations.

Numbers and Symbols

< > (angle brackets), placing HTML commands within, 190–191

/ (slash) character, use of in HTML commands, 191

321Gone, Web site, 240

A

About Me page, on eBay, 211

AcuBid.com, 240

Airborne Express rates, Web site, 163

Allied Shipping and Packaging Supplies, 159

Amazon

  accepting credit card payments through, **150–151**

  advice for a happy buying experience, **25**

  automatic extensions for hard outages of sites, 108

  Basic Information section, *169*

  bid increase increments for, 6

  fees for credit card payments, 150–151

  free storage of auction listing images by, 188

  guarantee, **26**

  Merchant Tools on, 212

  My Storefronts or zshops display pages, 211–212

  policies for ending auctions early, 104

  Seller's Tools for Success, 212

  steps for cancelling bids, 107

  timing the auction closing on, 199–204

  user feedback scoring system, 20

  Web site, 240

  Web site for bulk loader software, 203

Amazon.com, feedback page, *53*

American Box Company, 159

American Paper and Packaging, 159

America's Auctions and Sales, 240

angle brackets (<>), placing HTML commands within, 190–191

antiques, online price guide, 35

AOL Instant Messenger, using to communicate with bidders, 98

ArcSoft's PhotoStudio, editing digital images with, 185–186

asking price, costs included in, 8

A-to-z Guarantee, given by Amazon, 26

Auction 1 Online, 240

Auctionaddict.com, 240

Auction Booth, 211

  customizing in Yahoo!, **172–173**

  inserting a link to on the Yahoo! Auction page, 173

AuctionBuy, 240

Auction Express, bulk loader available on Yahoo!, 203

auction formats

  reasons for choosing each, 90

  table of types, 85

AuctionFun.com, 240

Auction Insights, 235

auction items. *See* online auction items

auction listings. *See* online auction listings

auction management programs

  checking your auctions with, 94

  on CD in book, 129

  using for record-keeping, 59

Auction Patrol, 235

auction policies, setting 214–220

Auction Port, 240

Auction Row, 235

auctions. *See* online auctions

Auctionscape, 240

Auctions.com, 240

Auction Trakker

  on CD in book, 39–41

  sniping, bidding, and record keeping software, 129

  using to snipe on eBay, **39–40**

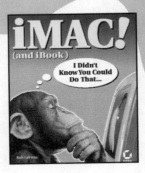